Captain of the Guild

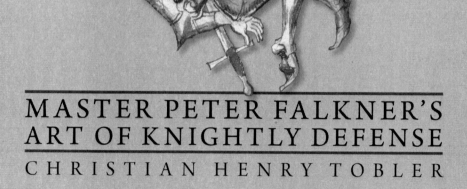

MASTER PETER FALKNER'S
ART OF KNIGHTLY DEFENSE

CHRISTIAN HENRY TOBLER

Freelance Academy Press, Inc.
www.FreelanceAcademyPress.com

Freelance Academy Press, Inc., Wheaton, IL 60189
www.freelanceacademypress.com

Black & White, Paperback Edition, 2012.

Printed in the United States of America
by Publishers' Graphics

21 20 19 18 17 16 15 14 13 12   1 2 3 4 5

ISBN 978-1-937439-09-5

Library of Congress Control Number: 2012952422

*To my wife Maureen, my parents Marilyn and Junius Tobler,
my students in the chapters of the Selohaar Fechtschule,
and to all those who seek wisdom in the sword.*

CONTENTS

PREFACE

Love at first sight

A couple of years ago, my dear friend and colleague Christian Tobler directed my attention to a codex he had started to work with. I must admit that I instantly fell in love with the Peter Falkner manuscript.

Being a native German speaker and an illustrator by profession, the illustrated German *Fechtbücher* have always had a considerable impact on me. Years ago, when I started to take interest in the authentic martial arts of our ancestors, there was hardly anything available to look at and learn from; apart from some very scarce online sources, there were only two or three black-and-white publications of which I was aware. Even under these less than perfect conditions the old codices did not fail to impress me deeply.

When Christian showed me the images of the Peter Falkner manuscript in full color, I could not help being immediately captivated by their splendor and brilliance. They may not be executed in as careful or meticulous a manner as the Paulus Kal figures or as the later specimens of Hans Talhoffer's beautifully illustrated manuscripts. But the style of Falkner's drawings is more to my personal taste than either those of Kal or Talhoffer—quite possibly because I am a quick and sketchy draftsman myself.

I got to know the Falkner manuscript rather late in my fencing career, which is a lucky and an unlucky circumstance at the same time. While I wish I could have spent more time admiring the illustrations, I quite likely might have been misled by them in my earlier days. Following the images to endeavor a recreation and reconstruction might have been an invitation too tempting to resist, and in hindsight, I am convinced that I was spared many a stray way. Only after having studied Master Johannes Liechtenauer's art of the longsword and other connected fighting and fencing disciplines of our forebears, do I have the hint of an idea as to what the often cryptic text wants to tell me. And being able to cross-check with a number of other sources is always a good idea, for Hauptmann Falkner's work is that of a master writing for others deeply immersed in his art.

The Falkner manuscript is truly remarkable. Among the surviving fencing treatises it forms an intriguing link between the older and the younger Liechtenauer-related sources. After all, the mysterious figure of Johannes Liechtenauer, a fencing master for whom we have no biographical data, overshadows the entire era of late medieval and early renaissance martial arts in old Germany. It is a satisfying circumstance that some of Liechtenauer's techniques are depicted with images, something the older sources from the beginning of the 15th century unfortunately do not offer. Master Falkner and another author by the name of Jörg Wilhalm have many images in common—occasionally the positions are so similar that it seems as if they were drawn from the same source by different artists. Also, there are strong parallels to other codices that are not explicitly linked to Master Liechtenauer and his teachings, e.g., the so-called Codex Wallerstein.

I am very thankful that Christian Tobler presents yet again an important piece of both martial and fine art to the wider audience of scholars and practitioners, and I do hope that with my little contribution of adding to the transcription I have helped to make it a well-deserved success.

As a matter of fact, it was Christian Tobler's first two books that helped me a lot when I left the path of sports fencing and redirected my steps into the vast new world of historical fencing. In a sense, I see dear Christian as some kind of martial Godfather. All the more I am happy, pleased, and flattered in having been asked to write some brief introductory words. Additionally, I am glad that finally I can return a favor Christian did for me when he wrote a preface to my own publication of the Peter von Danzig manuscript two years ago.

De gustibus non est disputandum, but for me the Falkner manuscript constitutes a peak among the old treatises. If I were to pick one out of the sixty-five surviving codices for my personal collection, the Falkner manuscript might quite probably be the one. Luckily, it is now available to everyone.

DIERK HAGEDORN
August, 2010

ACKNOWLEDGEMENTS

As always, it is impossible to thank everyone who had a part in the creation of this book. I will try however to make known those who were the most intimately involved.

I am forever indebted to my students, near and far, for their help in my research, diligence and enthusiasm in training, and unwavering support for the knightly arts. In particular, Jessica Finley and especially Aron Montaini have been very keen students of the Peter Falkner *Fechtbuch*, pointing out interesting techniques and adding their own interpretations of the book to our burgeoning body of knowledge. I'm sure Master Peter would be proud of them too.

I continue to profit from the generous collaboration of my friends and colleagues Dr. Jeffrey Forgeng, Paul S. Morgan Curator of the Higgins Armory Museum in Worcester, Massachusetts, and Mr. Dierk Hagedorn of the Hammaborg historical fencing organization in Hamburg, Germany. These two gentlemen did so much to strengthen both the transcription and translation of the manuscript.

A huge thank you goes out to the *Kunsthistorisches Museum* (KHM) in Vienna, Austria for allowing me to publish this book about a cherished part of their exquisite collection. I'd especially like to thank Ms. Ilse Jung and her staff for their kind cooperation regarding the manuscript images and for arranging permission for their use.

And I'd be remiss in not once again thanking my friends throughout the Western Martial Arts community: Nicole Allen, Jörg Bellinghausen, Claus Drexler, David Farrell, S. Matthew Galas, Bill Grandy, Stephen Hand, Maestro Sean Hayes, Hans Heim, the truly indispensable Stephen Hick, Keith Jennings, Craig Johnson, Christoph Kaindel, Peter Kautz, Alex Kiermayer, the late Norman Kidd, Jared Kirby, Jesse Kulla, Tom Leoni, Cecil Longino, Pamela Muir, Allen Reed, Steven Reich, David Rowe, Roger Siggs, Claus Sørensen, Thomas Stoeppler, Larry Tom, Jeff Tsay, Paul Wagner, Bart Walczak, Roland Warzecha, Theresa Wendland, William Wilson, Guy Windsor, and Grzegorz Zabinski. If I've forgotten some of you, please know you may have momentarily slipped out of my thoughts, but not my heart.

Jessica Finley, Bill Grandy, and Dierk Hagedorn did me the very great service of being readers for this book, and I am in their debt for this.

Lastly, I'd like to thank my partners at Freelance Academy Press: Greg Mele, Tom Leoni, and Adam Velez. Gentlemen, you make this stuff come alive.

ABOUT THE AUTHOR

Christian Henry Tobler has been a longtime student of swordsmanship, especially as it applies to the pursuit of the chivalric ideals. A passionate advocate of the medieval Liechtenauer School, his work in translating and interpreting Sigmund Ringeck's commentary firmly established him as an important contributor to the growing community of Western martial artists. This work is encapsulated in the 2001 title *Secrets of German Medieval Swordsmanship: Sigmund Ringeck's Commentaries on Johannes Liechtenauer's Verse*. A training guide for modern practitioners, *Fighting with the German Longsword*, followed in 2004. His 2006 book, *In Service of the Duke: The 15th Century Fighting Treatise of Paulus Kal*, is a facsimile, translation, and analysis of a lavishly illustrated Fechtbuch. Prior to this present volume, his most recent release was *In Saint George's Name: An Anthology of Medieval German Fighting Arts*, in 2010.

Mr. Tobler was born in 1963 in Paterson, New Jersey. A graduate of the University of Bridgeport's computer engineering program, Mr. Tobler has worked as a software developer, web designer, product manager, and marketing specialist in the analytical instrumentation and publishing fields. He is the Grand Master of the Order of Selohaar, an eclectic, mystic order of chivalry that he co-founded in 1979. A veteran of 20 years of tournament fighting, he is also an avid collector of reproduction arms and armour.

He has been focused on the study of medieval *Fechtbücher* (fight books) since the late 1990's. He has taught classes at the Schola St. George Swordplay Symposium, in the San Francisco Bay area, in Seattle at the Western Washington Western Martial Arts Workshop (4W), and at five of the Western Martial Arts Workshops (WMAW). He has also traveled the United States and Europe teaching numerous seminars, and has lectured at the 38th International Congress on Medieval Studies in Kalamazoo, Michigan.

Mr. Tobler lives in the United States, in rural Oxford, Connecticut, with his wife Maureen Chalmers, where he teaches a weekly class on medieval German combat, surrounded by far too many books and pieces of arms and armour for the size house that they live in.

THE SELOHAAR FECHTSCHULE

The **Selohaar** *Fechtschule* (German for "Fencing School") is a histori-cal fencing study group within the Order of Selohaar, an eclectic and mystic chivalric order. The group meets to research, study, and practice the martial arts of medieval and early Renaissance Europe under the guidance of its Principal Instructor, Christian Henry Tobler, an internationally-known researcher, instructor, and combatant who has instructed at seminars and sym-posia around the United States for eight years. Headquartered at its school in Connecticut, the Selohaar Fechtschule also has chapters in the states of Alaska, Florida, Kansas, New York, and Washington.

The Fechtschule focuses on the *Fechtbücher,* or "fight books," of the masters of the tradition arising from the teachings of the 14th-century grandmaster Johannes Liechtenauer. We use the treatises ascribed to Sigmund Ringeck, Peter von Danzig, Paulus Kal, Hans Talhoffer, Peter Falkner, and others, whose commentaries on Liechtenauer's secret verses constitute the medieval German *Kunst des Fechtens* (Art of Fighting). These manuscripts document the use of the longsword, messer, dagger, poleaxe, and unarmed combat, both in and out of armour, on foot and on horseback.

In addition to encouraging diligent training and scholarship, the Fechtschule and its parent organization stress the importance of good character through study of the Code of Chivalry and its original cultural milieu.

Website: http://www.selohaar.org/fechten.htm
E-mail: orderofselohaar@aol.com

INTRODUCTION

very martial culture throughout history has prized the trained warrior, eschewing mere brute force in favor of honed skill. Today's readers are acquainted with some of these warriors of the past, such as the Samurai and the fighting Shaolin monks. It is well known that these warriors trained using formalized martial arts. Less known is that the medieval knight was also a trained warrior. The movie-promulgated stereotype of the medieval knight is of the unskilled fighter, swinging clumsy blows and encumbered by weighty armour. This is a far cry from reality.

A fresh look at the knight in recent years has revealed a more refined image of these exemplars of the medieval warrior class. We know now that medieval armour was both a highly protective and very mobile defense; that knights trained from childhood for their profession; and, particularly through research of the last few decades, that they had access to sophisticated training methods. These fighting arts are every bit as effective and scientific in their approach as the martial arts of ancient Japan or China. The largest, though far from solitary, body of evidence supporting this last point comes to us from late medieval Germany.

The German fencing masters of the late Middle Ages have bequeathed to us a rich legacy of martial lore, enshrined in manuscripts detailing their fighting art in words and images. Numbered in the dozens, these works fall predominantly within the tradition of the shadowy 14th-century grandmaster Johannes Liechtenauer. A few hundred lines of mnemonic verse, opaque without the commentaries of his later (and fortunately, numerous) disciples, form the nucleus of his tradition.

The 15th century is the apogee of Liechtenauer's fighting art—a time when numerous fencing manuscripts were created and the fully armoured knight was still an important force on the battlefield. Masters such as Hans Talhoffer and Paulus Kal had sumptuously illustrated works created, often for noble patrons, or to impress would-be employers. Scribes created large compendium text manuscripts, grouping together the treatises of masters such as Sigmund Ringeck, the wrestler Ott the Jew, Martin Huntfeltz, Andres Lignitzer, Peter von Danzig, the

Jew Lew, and several variations of anonymous commentaries on Liechtenauer's own seminal verse. In the late 1470's, a cleric named Johannes Lecküchner would draw upon and modify Liechtenauer's teachings to create his own, mammoth volume on the falchion-like *messer*.

All these works have come to be known as *Fechtbücher*—"fight books"—and while the 16ᵗʰ and 17ᵗʰ centuries would see the continued creation of these books (some in print), they would be for a changing audience. In the twilight of the medieval knight, the fencing treatises would come to be aimed at a more bourgeois demographic and the growing body of printed works would make them widely available, rather than crafted for a single patron or student. So it is the 15ᵗʰ century that is the true period of the "knightly art," as Liechtenauer and his students dubbed it, though custom would ensure the continued use of that moniker for at least another century and half.

The subject of this volume, manuscript KK 5012, "Master Peter Falkner's Art of Knightly Defense," is a work from this time of transition at the end of the 15ᵗʰ century—an illustrated *Fechtbuch* by a master of the tradition engendered by Master Johannes Liechtenauer over a century earlier.

The Knightly Art

Liechtenauer left several hundred lines of cryptic, rhyming verses describing his fighting art. The verse was likely crafted with twin purposes in mind: to keep his teachings secret from outsiders, and to act as a mnemonic device for the student already inculcated in the art. Liechtenauer's verses expound chiefly upon his principal weapon, the *Langen Schwert*, or longsword. A descendant of the two-handed "great swords of war" of the 13ᵗʰ century, the longsword had a double-edged blade that tapered to a keen point, admirably suited to seeking the gaps in the increasingly sophisticated plate armours evolving throughout the 14ᵗʰ century.

The grandmaster's verse epitome, or *Zettel*, is divided into three parts. The first and longest section treats the use of the longsword without the protection of armour (*Bloßfechten*); it is here that most of Liechtenauer's terminology is established. This is followed by a shorter section specializing in mounted combat (*Roßfechten*); this is aimed at armoured judicial dueling and also includes methods for using the lance, as well as mounted wrestling techniques. A final section, the smallest of the three, deals with fighting in armour on foot (*Harnischfechten*); it too addresses the use of the lance or spear, and alludes briefly to the conclusion of such a duel on the ground, with daggers used to seek out the gaps in the armour.

There were other masters of the tradition who wrote commentaries, or glosses, which 'decode' Liechtenauer's verse. These glosses explain the meaning, usually through descriptions of techniques exemplifying the principles laid out in the verse. Still other masters, including Peter Falkner, added other weapons forms to this curriculum, such as the dagger, poleaxe, halberd, and the sword and buckler.

Falkner and the Marxbrüder

The *Fechtbuch* attributed to Peter Falkner is one of the last important 15th-century works of the Liechtenauer tradition. While it is undated, the clothing and armour shown throughout suggest the manuscript was created in the 1490's. The chronicle of the famed Marxbrüder fencing guild lends strength to this supposition, affirming Falkner's activity in the final years of the 15th century and the first of the 16th century.

The *Marxbrüder*, whose full name was the "Brotherhood of Our Dear Lady and Pure Virgin Mary and the Holy and Warlike Heavenly Prince Saint Mark," was granted the exclusive privilege of bestowing the title "Master of the Longsword" by the emperor Frederick III in 1487. The founding of the guild is a murkier matter however. The sword-bearing lion of St. Mark appears in Master Hans Talhoffer's 1459 codex, as it does here, on f. 57v of Falkner's work, but nothing survives to definitively link Talhoffer, or any other early Liechtenauer tradition master, with the guild. The earliest reliable trace is to 1474—several years after Talhoffer's final extant manuscript was created in 1467.

Falkner is mentioned several times in the guild's chronicle, itself contained within a 16th-century *Fechtbuch*,[1] not only as a member but, more significantly, as its elected *Hauptmann* (Captain), the title given to its leader. The chronicle lists him as being active prior to 1490 and mentions him in entries for the years 1496, 1504, and 1506. Two entries for 1502 attest to his being captain that year.[2]

Beyond these tantalizing scraps, little is left to us of the life and career of Peter Falkner. Where and when he was born, when he died, and how many years he was active are all things unknown. What we *do* know tells us that he was a fencing master of some importance, given the preeminence of the Marxbrüder guild at this time.

General Observations on the Manuscript

KK 5012, *Master Peter Falkner's Art of Knightly Defense*, is a paper manuscript of the late 15th century, now in the collection of the Kunsthistorisches Museum (KHM) in Vienna, Austria. Comprising 74 folia and bound to a leather, folder-style cover. The manuscript measures 208 x 137 mm. The paper is watermarked with a bunch of grapes; foliation, almost surely added well after the manuscript's creation, appears in the upper right corner of every tenth leaf. The water colored ink and pen drawings—save for a glued-in woodcut of the Crucifixion, a glued-in image of the lion of Saint Mark, and perhaps the more lavish art of folio 72v—seem to be the

---

[1] "Sigmund Schninig Fechtbuch," Cod.I.6.2°.5, Augsburg, 1539/1552, ff. 9v–10v.

[2] Hils, *Meister Johann Liechtenauers Kunst des Langen Schwert*, pp. 121–122.

work of a single artist. The text has been rendered by at least two scribes: the first is evident in folios 1v–46r, the second in folios 46v–72v. The initial letter of each line of verse or paragraph is struck through with a line of red ink.[3]

The manuscript includes illustrated fighting techniques for the longsword, messer, dagger, staff, halberd, poleaxe, dueling shield, and mounted combat.

The longsword and messer sections, which occupy over half the book, have only verse for their captions. In the longsword section, this verse is largely derived from the verse epitome, or *Zettel*, of Johannes Liechtenauer, the 14th-century grand-master and founder of the tradition of which Peter Falkner was a part. Falkner, or someone before him, has altered the verse in places. The verse for the *Messerfechten* (literally, "knife fighting") is taken from the huge treatise by the cleric Johannes Lecküchner; it too has been altered in some places, though with fewer divergences. The messer section is considerably longer than the preceding longsword portion, and is by far the manuscript's largest section.

The sections on the dagger, staff, halberd/poleaxe, dueling shield, and mounted combat are structured differently; while little bits of verse are at times included, the bulk of the text takes the form of descriptive paragraphs accompanying the illustrations. Additionally, the text appears to have been rendered by a different scribe[4] than the one who set down the longsword and messer sections. Each of the sections devoted to a particular weapon has a short preamble: for the dagger, staff, and axe, these appear on separate pages; for the dueling shield and mounted combat, these are short paragraphs atop the first illustrated page of the section.

The inclusion of verse for the first two parts of the manuscript might at first seem peculiar when compared to the other parts which have paragraphs. However, Dr. Jeffrey Forgeng of the Higgins Armory Museum remarked to me that this was likely so simply because there *isn't* any verse for the other sections. The verse epitome for the longsword was always a staple of the of the Liechtenauer tradition, and by the end of the 15th century Lecküchner's *Messerfechten* verse had achieved almost equal prominence. No such verse survives, however, for the dagger, shield, or other weapons.

---

[3]   All physical data on the manuscript is drawn from: Rainer Leng (compiler), *Katalog der deutschsprachigen illustrierten Handschriften des Mittelalters*, Band 4/2, Lieferung 1/2–38. Fecht- und Ringbücher. C. H. Beck'sche Verlagsbuchhandlung, 2008 pp. 18–20.

[4]   A third scribe may have written the dagger preamble.

• Contents of Manuscript KK 5012

The Manuscript in Detail

• *The Longsword* (ff. 1v–18r)

The longsword section is perhaps the most challenging portion of Falkner's book, and as such it demands the most inspection and analysis. Verse is used to caption the images and, as noted earlier, this is a combination of Liechtenauer's verse, Falkner's changes to it, and portions culled from Lecküchner's verse for the *messer*. Sometimes, the illustrations appear to be quite different from earlier ones of the Liechtenauer canon, or from the descriptions found in the major surviving glosses, or commentaries, that are reproduced copiously in the 15th- and 16th-century *Fechtbücher*.

The longsword is the principal weapon of this tradition, so it is no surprise to find it given pride of place in Falkner. However, it is my belief that Falkner is first and foremost a "messer man," given the number of importations and adaptations of Lecküchner's techniques for that weapon into the longsword section. Examples of this include the *Sonnen Zaigen;*[5] or "Sun Pointer" (f. 14v), a form of takedown; an adaptation of a sword entrapment (f. 15r); and a counter to the "Hanging Point" (f. 16v). At other times, the messer verse supplants the usual Liechtenauer verse; examples of this may be found in folios 9r–10v, 14r, 15v, 17r, and 17v. Folios 15r and 16r feature use of the *Gewappnet* or "armed [hand]" grip, known elsewhere in the tradition as "half-sword" or "shortened sword." This grip has the left hand holding the middle of the blade, hearkening to both Liechtenauer's armoured combat, as well as a number of Lecküchner's messer techniques.

---

[5]   The *Sonnen Zaigen's* evolution in the *Fechtbücher* is a convoluted one: its earliest appearance is as a grappling technique performed on horseback; it is included in Liechtenauer's mounted combat verse. Lecküchner adapted it for use on foot with the messer, with Falkner then folding it into the longsword techniques.

Furthering the impression of the messer's pre-eminence in Falkner's *Fechtbuch* is his listing of *six* strokes for the longsword. He adds the everyday *Oberhau* (Stroke from Above) to Liechtenauer's list of "Five Secret Strokes." Given the *Oberhau* is a simple stroke, this looks suspiciously like an attempt to harmonize the longsword teachings with those for the messer, which in Lecküchner's text does indeed include six special strokes.

The earlier portion of the longsword section (ff. 1v–8v) should be familiar to students of Liechtenauer's longsword teachings, though it too is not without its eccentricities. Falkner shortens and changes Liechtenauer's prologue (not in itself an uncommon practice) and then goes on to list his six strokes. The verse for the *Oberhau* on folio 2r is both familiar and revised:

> *Mark what I say to you: a stroke from above strike true*
> *And left against right should you strongly fight[6]*
> *Also you can therein hang, and the thrust bring*

While the second line is drawn directly from Liechtenauer, the first and third lines appear to be Falkner's innovation.

This pattern continues in both verse and illustration throughout the longsword section. The *Zornhau* (Wrath Stroke) on folio 2v also uses hybridized verse, stressing a concept not seen earlier in the canon: the idea of performing the blow with or without an accompanying step. The illustration is also interesting, for it shows the fighter in a low stance, seemingly striking to his opponent on the outside of his attack, rather than interrupting it. Whether the illustration represents the primary action, or follow-on technique, such as an *Abnehmen* (Taking Off) to the other side of the opponent's sword, is uncertain.

Other interesting divergences figure beyond this. In the *Krumphau* (Crooked Stroke) plate (f. 4v), the swordsman is binding his opponent's blade with a left foot lead, rather than the wide, outward step of the right foot advocated in the common glosses. Hans Talhoffer's version[7] of this same image, in his 1467 illustrated work, has some of this quality, but it seems more pronounced here. The *Zwerchhau* (Thwart Stroke) on folio 5r has the combatant stepping with his right foot to outside his opponent's right foot. This is intriguing, for the picture resembles some footwork in Lecküchner's messer work, but there too, the illustrations are sometimes at variance with the text. The surviving glosses

---

[6] This is a very significant though, without explanation, cryptic verse. It describes the virtues of beginning with the left foot leading and then stepping with the right foot forward during the stroke.

[7] Hans Talhoffer, *Fechtbuch*, Munich, 1467, f. 11r.

describe the *Zwerchhau* as incorporating a step away from the attacker's blow, so this plate may represent an innovation on Falkner's part, or some illustrational anomaly; in lieu of descriptive paragraphs, it is impossible to know for sure. A possible explanation may lie in the image on folio 6r, where a second Zwerchhau to the right side is performed with the victor having pivoted all but behind his opponent's back; certainly the footwork of f. 5r would facilitate this follow-up.[8]

Another follow-on play of the *Zwerchhau* (f. 5v) features a strange illustration. The verse describes striking the *Zwerchhau* to the four openings, which correspond to the guards *Ochs* and *Pflug*, on either side; that is, we are to target high and low on both sides. Curiously though, what is illustrated is not this mode of attack, but the guards *Ochs* and *Pflug* themselves. Stranger still is that the guards are never given their own exposition in the longsword section, though that is not the case in the messer section.

The illustration of the *Schielhau*, or "Squinting Stroke," on folio 7r has drawn considerable interest among researchers, particularly Claus Sørensen of the Laurentiusgildet historical fencing school in Århus, Denmark.[9] It seems to imply a very powerful deflection has occurred *prior* to the wielder hitting his opponent, rather than a relatively simultaneous deflection and counterstroke. Such depictions of the *Schielhau* appear in some of the 16th-century *Fechtbücher* attributed to Jörg Wilhalm; perhaps Wilhalm was drawing upon Falkner.[10]

Also arcane is Falkner's verse for the last of the five "Secret Strokes"—the *Scheitelhau*, or "Scalp Stroke":

> *The Scalper is a danger to the head*
> *Then strike it through below with three steps*
> *Four strikes make from both sides*

There is no analogue to this advice in the earlier treatises, so precisely what it is that Falkner is advocating is unclear from his rather opaque verse.[11]

---

[8]   My students in Kansas, Jessica Finley and Aron Montaini, and Hammaborg's Dierk Hagedorn independently came up with this same observation. I am indebted to them for this contribution.

[9]   My thanks to Mr. Sørensen for sharing his research on and interpretations of the *Schielhau*.

[10]   Less likely, though far from impossible, is that the reverse is true. If Wilhalm's works date from *late* in his life, it is possible that it is Falkner who was inspired by him.

[11]   Perhaps, as Dierk Hagedorn has proposed, this alludes to not only the Scheitelhau itself, but also its potential follow-on actions: the winding following the opponent's parry in the *Kron* (Crown) position, slicing under his arms, and the withdrawal from danger following the slice. These in turn could involve a total of four steps accompanying the action.

Another instance where Jörg Wilhalm may have followed Falkner (or some related work) is Falkner's depiction of the *Sprechfenster* ("Speaking Window"), a tactical application of the guard *Langenort*, or "Long Point"—a guard held with the point extended against the opponent. Falkner's verse for this technique closely follows Liechtenauer's, but he shows a very interesting grip on the sword: the left hand is reversed. Such a grip appears elsewhere, including the 1467 Fechtbuch by Master Hans Talhoffer,[12] and in the anonymous "Codex Wallerstein," a compendium manuscript of the 15th century.

Experimentation, notably that spearheaded by Dierk Hagedorn of the Hammaborg historical fencing association in Hamburg, Germany, has shown that this position offers some unique mechanical advantages. More exploration is still needed to fully understand the application of this grip, but this recent research is already driving a radical shift away from the older view that the illustrations of this grip were artistic errors or flights of fancy.

Perhaps a better candidate for an artistic error is the illustration on folio 10r. Here, the figures are either purposefully rendered as left-handed (a unique occurrence in the manuscript) or the image has been somehow inverted. Perhaps the artist copied an earlier image incorrectly?

The longsword section concludes with the words "Here ends Master Peter Falkner's art with the longsword." This is worthy of discussion because the modern reader sees this and, knowing that the work derives from Liechtenauer and Lecküchner, is tempted to accuse the Hauptmann of plagiarism. However, we must remember that period fencing masters copied from each other freely. Further, this is Falkner's own collection of techniques—the things he feels are important to show. But certainly, we mustn't imagine Falkner attempting to fool anyone into thinking this is all his invention: the Liechtenauer corpus would have been well-known to his fellow guildsmen. Rather, to modern sensibilities this verse tells us that this is Master Peter Falkner's personal expression of the larger tradition.

---

[12] Hans Talhoffer, *Fechtbuch*, Cod. Icon 394a, Munich, 1467, f. 17r.

• Messer (ff. 18v–43v)

The *messer* is the second most prominent weapon of the Liechtenauer tradition. Simply meaning 'knife', in some treatises this does refer to a typical knife, but more often in this context it is the 'big knife' that is described: a falchion-like sword, but built with a hilt of knife-like scale construction. Such weapons could be workmanlike, while others were elaborately decorated for wealthier owners. These could be as long as a sword, and two-handed versions are known among surviving pieces. Fighting messers usually featured a slightly curved blade with a thick spine and a clipped point, the abbreviated false edge often sharpened. A metal projection off of the hilt, called the *Wernagel* ("weapon nail"), provided additional protection for the hand.

The messer is mentioned in the earliest known manuscript containing fight lore of the Liechtenauer tradition, Hs. 3227a,[13] sometimes called the *Nürnberger Hausbuch* ("Nuremberg Housebook"). Alas, the text is brief here, and it is difficult to know whether it was intended as general advice, or if the original intent was for it to serve as a prologue for a longer segment that was never completed. The section begins thus:

> As the sword is taken and founded in the long messer, whoever wishes to learn to fight with the messer should first note and know that the fundamentals and principals that apply to the sword also apply to the messer.

> A man has but two hands and has from each hand two strikes above and two below. From them come thrusts and slices, as with the sword, with the winding. [...]

---

[13]   At least this is the common wisdom: Hs. 3227a has been dated to 1389, based upon a calendar also contained in this *housebook*—a sort of medieval "home encyclopedia." The calendar however may, or may not, reflect the manuscript's date of creation.

The writer here draws a connection between the methods for fighting with the sword and messer. This stressing of a holistic approach to fighting is not unique to this passage—the connections between wrestling and fencing, and between the staff and sword, are also lauded elsewhere in Hs. 3227a. And, as will see later, such sentiments are not unique to this early source.

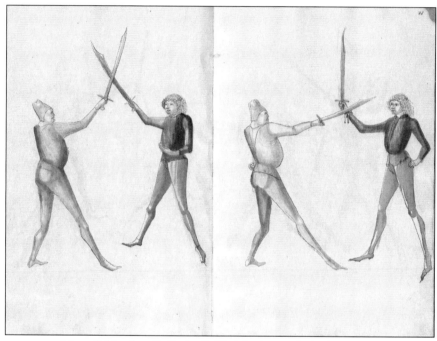

Messer fighting from the Paulus Kal Fechtbuch, a pre-Lecküchner source.
KHM, Vienna, KK 5126, ff. 77v & 78r.

The messer appears throughout the German fencing manuscripts of the 15th century, usually in relatively short collections of techniques. Masters Hans Talhoffer, Paulus Kal, and an anonymous author within the Codex Wallerstein all feature methods for fighting with this smaller, but formidable weapon.

But by the late 15th century, the *Messerfechten* treatise by the cleric Johannes Lecküchner had joined the constellation of recurring works included in the manuscripts of the Liechtenauer tradition, by and large displacing the earlier masters' messer techniques. Beginning with two enormous manuscripts attributed to Lecküchner himself, one a text-only version from 1478, the other an illustrated edition from 1482, this treatise is featured regularly in many of the compendia that follow, sometimes as a whole, at other times in parts. Peter Falkner culls selections from Lecküchner material to populate his own messer fighting section.

In contrast to his liberties with the longsword material, Falkner's adherence to the messer canon is much stronger, and the plates closely follow Lecküchner's illustrations and verse; any divergences are small. Falkner begins with a prologue which closely follows Lecküchner's own (though it omits two lines):

If you are eager
to strive for messer fighting
then learn the art that adorns you
in play and in earnest combat

Falkner follows Lecküchner's ordering of techniques, beginning with the messer's six strokes (ff. 18v–23v), sometimes including multiple techniques for each, although this is still a small subset of Lecküchner's diverse assortment. The first of these strokes has the same name as its longsword counterpart: the *Zornhau*, or "Wrath Stroke." This is followed by the *Weckerhau* (Awakening Stroke), an analogue to the longsword *Krumphau*; the *Entrüsthau* (Disarming Stroke), the messer version of the *Zwerchhau*; the *Zwingerhau* (Constraining Stroke), which is akin to the *Schielhau*; and the *Geferhau* (Danger Stroke), which is the messer equivalent to the longsword's *Scheitelhau*. A sixth blow is included by Lecküchner, and Falkner after him—the *Winckerhau*, or "Winking Stroke," a blow delivered with the false, or short, edge to one side, then the other.

The four guards for the messer—analogues to those for the longsword—appear on folios 24r–24v, though the latter two are accompanied by the verse for the "Four Oppositions" (*Vier Versetzen*) that counter the guards. As with the longsword, there are two 'open' positions inviting attack and two 'closed' stances that close the lines of attack. The guards *Luginslant* (Watchtower) and *Pastei* (Bastion)[14] are depicted on folio 24r; these are open guards that are equivalent to the longsword guards of *vom Tag* (from the Roof) and *Alber* (Fool), respectively. The two closed guards follow on folio 24v; they are the *Eber* (Boar) and *Stier* (Steer), which equate to the *Pflug* (Plow) and *Ochs* (Ox) of the longsword.

The plates that follow go on to show techniques familiar from the longsword curriculum, such as *Ansetzen* (Planting), *Nachreisen* (Chasing), *Überlaufen* (Overrunning), *Abschneiden* (Slicing Off), *Absetzen* (Setting Off), *Durchwechseln* (Changing Through), *Zucken* (Pulling), *Durchlaufen* (Running Through), as well as messer-specific techniques such as the *Bogen* (Bow) and *Scorpian* (Scorpion). Along the way, various arm locks, pommel strokes, and takedowns appear, all drawn from the verse of Johannes Lecküchner. An adaptation of the half-sword grip, called out as the *Gewappnet* ("armed") hand or point, again derives from Lecküchner's work and appears here on folios 39r, 39v, and 43v.

---

[14]   Note that the illustrations are ordered differently than the verse. This is also true on the following page for the other two guards.

Clumsily scrawled lines disapprovingly cross out the images on folios 33v and 42v. At first glance at least, these seem to be contemporary with the manuscript, so perhaps the artist or Master Peter himself felt they contained errors. Certainly, the image of folio 33v does not accord well with the image or description found in Lecküchner, but it's difficult to make such an argument regarding 42v. Given this, there's no clear answer as to why these cross-outs appear.

Folio 38v begs some scrutiny, as Falkner may be garbling Lecküchner's original intent. The plate shows the defender about to draw his messer from its scabbard, but Lecküchner's text makes clear this set of verses treats the situation where you must ward off an attack *unarmed*. The first line of verse is where the important variation lies: Lecküchner begins with "If you go without a weapon" (*Gestu an were*),[15] but Falkner renders this as "If you have a weapon" (*Hastu ain wer*). A scribal error at some point could explain this variance, but it is also possible that Falkner intended to convey a different idea. The 1459 Hans Talhoffer *Fechtbuch* in Copenhagen has an illustration of a very similar technique that begins with the sword sheathed and such a technique is described in an anonymous messer treatise contained in the early 16th-century *Fechtbuch* now in Glasgow.

• *Crucifixion Scene* (f. 44r)

A somber vignette of the Crucifixion, rendered on a separate small leaf applied to the page, appears on folio 44r. This follows immediately after the conclusion of the messer section and is followed by three blank pages. Seemingly the work of a different artist, it shows a profusely bleeding Christ proffered vinegar as he suffers on the cross, with several other biblical figures looking on. The painting is crude, with the colors exceeding the outlines. The Latin inscription *IHS Nazarenus Rex Iudeorum* ("Jesus of Nazareth, King of the Jews") captions the picture above.

---

[15] Johannes Lecküchner, "Fechtbuch," Cgm 582, Munich, 1482, f. 136r.

• Dagger (ff. 46r–56r)

Falkner's section on the dagger is a delightfully unique occurrence among the medieval German *Fechtbücher*, for it combines illustrations with substantial and clear text. Much of the standard repertoire found in text sources such as the *Von Danzig Fechtbuch* or in illustrated sources like those of Paulus Kal or Hans Talhoffer is presented here, only this time with both words and pictures.

Folio 46r has no illustration but contains instead a prologue, strangely geared towards armoured judicial combat, which doesn't seem to be the focus of the plates that follow:

Here begins the dagger fighting in harness. If you want this to be secret, then if he falls wrench a large piece from his coat armour and thrust it into his visor with the dagger, thus you see to it that he cannot free himself. This is good when it is sandy, thus one wins a great advantage.

The use of the word "secret" (*verborgen*) in this passage is significant, for we read often in the *Fechtbücher* of "secret" or "forbidden" techniques which are not meant to be taught at public fencing and are intended only for serious, deadly encounters.

The section is noteworthy for its inclusion of techniques not featured elsewhere in the 15th century Liechtenauer canon. The techniques for the upper and lower "shields"—techniques where the dagger is held with the left hand bracing the blade, not unlike the half-sword—are presented with conclusions left vague by, say, Master Talhoffer. Here, both the Upper Shield (f. 48r) and Lower Shield (f. 51r) are used to disarm the opponent. The counter to a "long thrust" on folio 47v is also unique to Falkner. So is the "Figure 4 Lock" of folio 50r; this is similar to one of Master Paulus Kal's plays, but performed by beginning in a high guard rather than the lower one.

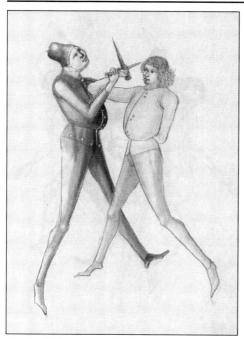

Paulus Kal's version of the 'Figure 4 Lock' with the dagger. KHM, Vienna, KK 5126, f. 84r.

Pay close attention to folio 54v. The text and illustration are in disagreement here: they describe the action on opposite sides of the body. Practice with this technique points to the illustration being in error, for the attacker is unlikely to be stabbing low with his left foot forward as he breaks wide measure to attack. The text is therefore the more likely to be accurate.

The section, eminently useful to the martial artist for its rich and complete content, ends with two interesting techniques. The first of these, on folio 55v, is a "Full Nelson" hold put onto an opponent who has gained control of both daggers. The second, on folio 56r, shows a hold on the ground, such as those described for armoured combat following a takedown. The latter is also remarkable for featuring an obscure little 'x' in the margin; such annotations also appear among the dagger techniques on folios 46v, 48r, 50v, and 51r. The intent of these is as equally mysterious as the cross-outs in the messer section.

• *The Lion of St. Mark* (f. 57v)

Like the crucifixion scene in folio 44r, this image of the lion of St. Mark looks to be a separate leaf of paper applied to the page. The lion, his head surrounded by a golden nimbus, clutches a sword. The presence of this sigil, used by the *Marxbrüder* as their emblem, is an indication of Peter Falkner's role in that organization.

• Staff Fighting (ff. 58r–61r)

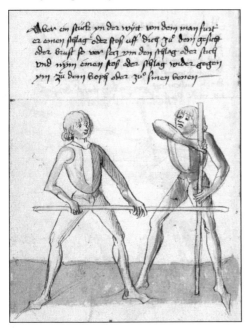

While arguably the foundation for all fighting with long-hafted weapons, the staff isn't featured prominently in 15th-century German *Fechtbücher*. Falkner is one of the first to devote much space to it, although he only includes six techniques. In the Liechtenauer tradition, the staff is first alluded to in Hs. 3227a, but the section meant to address it was seemingly never completed—only what must surely be a prologue is present:

Whoever wishes to learn to fight with the staff should first know and note that a proper staff should be twelve spans[16] long, and that fighting with the staff is taken from the sword. And as one fights with the sword, so shall he fight also with the staff. And the principles that apply to the sword, such as before, after, bravery, quickness, wile, prudence, etc., apply also to the staff.[17]

The anonymous author, writing in this early Liechtenauer source takes great pains to instruct that the staff employs the same basic principles as the sword. This same idea of reminding the reader that one weapon is much like another is reflected in another late 15th-century work, an anonymous poleaxe treatise, included in the addenda of the Vienna copy of the Paulus Kal *Fechtbuch*. Here, it is the staff that is used as a basis for the axe:

Item: do thus to fight with the battleaxe: learn to bind above and below as with the staff.

---

16   A *span* is the width of the outstretched hand; usually, approximately 9 inches. This yields a staff roughly nine feet in length.

17   Anonymous Housebook, Hs. 3227a, Nuremberg, c. 1389?, f. 78r.

Falkner's own prologue for the staff, which is written in verse, does not explicitly liken it to other weapons, but instead exposits a series of fundamentals, shared by all:

> Note what I say:
> be quick with the staff,
> winding and lifting,
> fighting and laying down.
> Do not forget the plunging down,
> also do the five strokes,
> with falling over and from the winding,
> also learn to find strokes and thrusts.

The "five strokes"[18] mentioned here are likely a series of strokes for the sword... but which set of five? There are the "Five Secret Strokes" of Liechtenauer's teachings for the longsword—the *Zornhau*, *Krumphau*, *Zwerchhau*, *Schielhau*, and *Scheitelhau*. However, there is another list of five strokes, one that runs in parallel with Liechtenauer's secret blows, that describes basic trajectories of hewing strokes with the sword; these are the *Oberhau* (Stroke from Above), *Unterhau* (Stroke from Below), *Mittelhau* (Middle Stroke), *Wechselhau* (Changing Stroke), and *Sturzhau* (Plunging Stroke).

While it's impossible to be sure, the likelihood is that this refers to the latter list, for when there are five blows listed for a weapon besides the longsword, they are those of the second list. Examples of this are the description of the blows with the dueling shield found in the *Gladiatoria* manuscript, a mostly armoured combat work, now in Krakow, and in five of the six plays for the sword and buckler associated with Master Andres Lignitzer, which figure in numerous Liechtenauer manuscripts. Additionally, the *Wechselhau* is called out explicitly in the first play as a position from which to begin—presumably one has struck this blow and now starts from its terminus.

Six techniques for the staff follow the verse prologue; their wording is at times opaque, and open to considerable interpretation. The first, as said above, uses a low-lying position (the *Wechselhau*, or "Change Stroke") to begin the action. What's very interesting is that this play begins with two lines of verse giving general advice—"If you want to act with discipline, you should attend to the four bindings"—which harkens to the idea of first needing to bind above and below, per

---

[18] The wider meaning of the German word "hau" is clear here. It means "stroke" or "hewing blow" (and "hau" and "hew," its English cognate, have a common origin), but the word "cut" would be too specific a translation; obviously, staves do not cut.

the anonymous poleaxe treatise cited above. In any case, the idea of the technique is to come up from below and bind staves, with another bind following if your opponent strikes around to renew his assault.

The remaining five techniques include methods for jamming the opponent's attack by striking over his shoulder (f. 59r), called "Overrunning"; holding the staff in a vertical position to parry (f. 59v); a nasty disarming technique (f. 60r), effected by squeezing his hands between both staves, called "the Clamp"; an application of *Winden* ("winding") principles (f. 60v); and a takedown over the leg in a technique called "Underrunning" (f. 61r).

The last technique is a little unclear, and all the more so because the text advises one to place "your left foot behind his"; unless there's a word ("right") missing after "his," then the illustration confounds the text. This wouldn't be unprecedented, given one of the dagger plays discussed earlier.

• *Halberd and Poleaxe* (ff. 62r–65r)

Following the six staff plays are six for the varying forms of poleaxe and halberd. As with the staff, the illustrated plates are preceded by a brief prologue on f. 62r, describing what is to come, and its application:

Note this is also a lesson of how you should, with dueling weapons, act with the murder axe and the halberd, which is also for the judicial duel, striking, thrusting and wrestling counter-techniques.

This introduction makes clear there is little or no difference between how one fights with a halberd and a poleaxe; in this sentiment Falkner is consistent with numerous other authors of early fencing treatises. It is also clear that the techniques of this section are specifically for judicial dueling, and *armoured* judicial dueling at that, as the plates depict. The combatants in each plate wear typical late 15th-century armours.

The "murder axe" (*Mordt Agst*) referenced here is usually reckoned by modern arms and armour authorities to be a long-hafted, broad, often crescent-shaped, axe, with a top spike and an abbreviated spike opposite the large blade. However, the artist interchanges polearms throughout the six plates, sometimes illustrating what appear to be halberds, hammer-headed poleaxes, and even what might be more properly termed a bill.

Adding further to the sense that the author feels "a pole arm is a pole arm" is that the variety of staff-mounted weapons can't be correlated with the specific names used in each play. In the first play (f. 62v), for instance, we're told how to act when "you have a murder axe or halberd in the hand," but one of the combatants is armed with a hammer-headed poleaxe—what the German masters would call a *Streitaxst*, or "battle axe." The term *Streitaxst* (renderd in this manuscript as "*strytt agst*") itself appears in the fifth play (f. 64v), but the two antagonists' weapons appear to be a bill and a halberd. So there seems to be little concern with these details, the various staff weapons being largely interchangeable.

The six plays for the axe are a very significant set of data points for those interpreting German poleaxe combat, for half of them describe methods not seen elsewhere in the Liechtenauer tradition's extant body of works. The first play on f. 62v describes an action which starts in a point-forward guard at the side, akin to longsword's *Pflug* guard, but which sweeps upward with the butt of axe to parry a downward blow; the plate shows this parry effected in such a way that the opponent's leading hand is entangled.

The second play (f. 63r) is a bit less novel: it shows a high defense with the haft of the axe—a setup for several potential follow-on actions. The third play (f. 63v) is also found elsewhere; one parries with the tail of the axe, and then swings the axe's head up and around from below to place it at the opponent's neck to throw him.

The fourth play (f. 64r) is also unique and describes a parry performed at the side of the body, after which follows a thrust from the bottom spike. More prosaic is the fifth technique's (f. 64v) counter to an attempted takedown, with the attacker's axe at the defender's neck, where the defender is advised to use the haft of his axe to push the elbow of his foe away, thwarting the throw.

The sixth and last play, on f. 65r, employs a delightful bit of deceit. The attacker is told to feint an attack to the head—"prepare a great stroke," as the text has it—but then pull his blow when his opponent reacts by raising his axe to parry. The play ends with a thrust below this mistaken parry. In the illustration, one can almost see the disappointment on the deceived defender's face!

• Dueling Shield (ff. 65v–67r)

In historical fencing treatises, likely nothing looks as strange to the uninitiated as the man-sized dueling shields. Often shown festooned with hooks, barbs, and spikes, these exotic shields could be swung with both hands, thrust at an opponent, or used to drag him off his feet. However, despite their evocation of some strange weapon of science fiction, dueling shields are mainstays of the 15th-century *Fechtbücher*; they're featured in every edition of Hans Talhoffer, Paulus Kal's c. 1470 work, the Codex Wallerstein, the Krakow version of the *Gladiatoria* manuscript, and more.

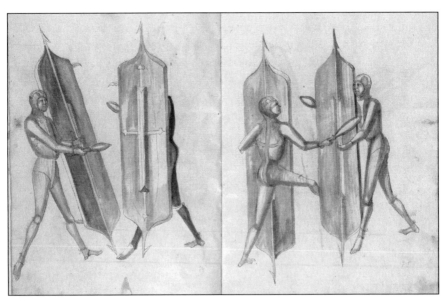

Dueling shield combat from the Paulus Kal Fechtbuch in Vienna. KHM, Vienna, KK 5126, f. 50r.

Two forms of combat with the dueling shield can be discerned from the fight books. Talhoffer shows both: the Swabian Rite, fought with shield and sword, and the Franconian Rite, fought with the shield and a mace-like club. The latter, named for the region and original German "stem duchy"[19] of Franconia, seems to be the form of combat used in Bavaria during the 15th century, likely because by this time the latter's borders incorporated much of that older territory. Perhaps because of this, the Bavarian master Paulus Kal shows only the club form. Falkner too is satisfied to depict only this form; perhaps this tells us something about his location, or the circles he moved in.

Following a brief preamble—*Note, this is an accurate report of the Franconian duel with shield, club and dagger counter-techniques*—Falkner goes on to show a small sampling of techniques; a mere four in all. The first simply describes the tactic of separating the opponent from his shield after he has thrown his club at you, which you've deflected with your shield, naturally. The second technique involves a thrust between his arms and behind his shield. The third involves a desperate measure—parrying a shield attack with the dagger following the loss of our own shield and club. The final technique on folio 67r is a grapple that begins with both combatants reduced to wielding only their daggers.

Take note of the ever-growing pile of discarded weapons at the feet of the duelists as the techniques progress. This is a common motif in *Fechtbücher* showing judicial duels involving multiple weapons.

• *Mounted Combat* (ff. 67v–72v)

The final section of the manuscript covers *Roßfechten*, or mounted combat. Falkner's equestrian combat techniques closely follow a combination of those illustrated in various sources—such as the Talhoffer and Kal manuscripts—and those described in the commentaries on Liechtenauer's *Roßfechten*. Save for the mounted wrestling methods and one "pursuit" technique, each plate for the sword or lance is associated with a given starting guard position.

---

[19] These duchies, dating from the 9th century, were Bavaria, Franconia, Lotharingia, Saxony, and Swabia.

Following the ordering of the Liechtenauer commentaries, the lance is treated first. A short, functional prologue begins the text for the first plate:

> *Here begins Master Peter Falkner's art on horseback, first with the lance, thereafter with the sword and with wrestling. This is the text of a general lesson on horseback.*

The first guard is described on folio 67v. The lance is held couched under the right armpit, and the reader is instructed to disengage under his opponent's lance as the two riders close with each other, hitting him on the opposite side. This is an application of the longsword principle of *Durchwechseln*, or "Changing Through."

The second guard has the lance held with both hands, low on the left side of the horse, seemingly out of play. Falkner's second guard is akin to the *third* lance guard described in the anonymous commentaries on Liechtenauer's mounted combat, found in the Von Danzig Fechtbuch:

> *Use this from the third guard thus: when you ride to each other, then hold your lance with both hands in the middle across before you on the saddlebow. If he rides to you with his lance, then slash with the forward part of your lance to his right side onto his lance, and thereupon strike your lance under your right armpit and ride on; thus you hit and he does not. Also, from all three guards you should come with the left hand to help on the lance if you want more strength.[20]*

In both cases, Falkner's version and that of the commentaries, as the opponent approaches, the lance is lifted up to strike the opponent's aside, placing one's own point at the same time. This is analogous to the *Absetzen*, or "Setting Aside," of the longsword teachings—an action that at once parries an opponent's attack and thrusts to him.

The third guard is held with the butt of the lance trailing on the ground on the right side of the horse. As the riders close the lance is then thrust forward, simultaneously driving the opponent's weapon aside and hitting him with the point.

The fourth guard is rather curiously labeled, for it is not a guard for the lance, but rather one to use with the sword *against* the lance. The sword is held across the horse's neck, and then struck to the right side to parry the incoming lance and thrust into the oncoming rider's face. This too is represented in the Von Danzig commentaries:

---

[20] "Von Danzig Fechtbuch," Codex 44 A 8, Rome, 1452, f. 40v.

...if he rides to your right side, then slash straight up with your sword to his lance to your right side. And go up into the upper hanging and set [the point] upon him to his face[21]

Folio 69v contains a technique for when one is being pursued by another rider. The lance is held over the shoulder, preventing the opponent from closing. The victor then turns his horse sharply around to the left, bringing the lance to bear against his pursuer. This technique is a staple of both the commentaries and various illustrated sources, such as those attributed to Masters Kal and Talhoffer; it is associated with the couplet from Liechtenauer's *Roßfechten* verse: *If one charges on the right, Turn around; tend to the fight.* The gloss from the Von Danzig manuscript explains the verse, further supporting Falkner's own description:

Note, when you are charging away from him and you have a lance and he does also, and he charges after you, then hold your lance on your right shoulder. And note, when he comes almost to you from behind, then raise your lance over your head on your left shoulder and turn against him to your left side and therewith strike your lance under your arm. Thus you come to him therewith straight under his eyes.[22]

This pursuit technique is not limited to the Liechtenauer tradition. The early 15th century works of the Italian master Fiore dei Liberi also describe something very similar:

The Master who is fleeing isn't armoured; while his horse runs fast, he throws backwards thrusts at his opponent. If he turned to his right, he'd be in Dente di Cinghiaro (Boar's Tooth), if he turned to his left, he would be in Posta di Donna (Woman's Guard); he could parry and strike as in the first and third plays of the lance.[23]

Moving to the fight of the sword against the sword, Falkner includes another short introductory statement, which continues the theme of describing the techniques according to their starting guards:

Here begins the art of the sword on horseback. If you want to fight masterfully with it then you should know before all things the three guards.

---

[21] ibid, ff. 48v – 49r.

[22] ibid, f. 48v.

[23] Fiore dei Liberi, "Fior di Battaglia," M.S. Ludwig XV 13, Getty Museum, Los Angeles, 1409, f. 42r. Translation, Tom Leoni.

The commentaries often have four or five guards, but Falkner contents himself with only three: one held across the body, with the blade cradled on the left (bridle) arm; a second held like the longsword guard *Pflug*, low and slanting up at the opponent at the right side; and a third held high at the right like the longsword guard *Ochs*. All three guards appear in the mainstream Liechtenauer commentaries, usually supplemented by a half-sword guard and one with the pommel of the sword resting on the pommel of the saddle. Paulus Kal's illustrated *Fechtbuch* also has a guard like *vom Tag*, with the sword held high, ready to strike down from above. The three guards match well the first three of five described in the Von Danzig commentaries, the only difference lying in the ordering of the second and third guards:

This is the First Guard
When you sit upon the horse, then hold your sword with your right hand by the grip and lay it with the blade on your left arm.

This is the Second Guard
When you sit upon the horse, then hold your sword with your right hand to your right side up above your head and hang the point toward his face.

This is the Third Guard
When you sit upon the horse, then hold your sword with your right hand beside your right leg so that the point stands toward your opponent.[24]

From the first guard, on folio 70r, we're told to drive up from the cradled position onto the opponent's sword to set off his stroke or thrust. On the next page, and starting from the second guard, the advice is to threaten a thrust, drawing a parry from the opponent; once he parries, the hilt is driven around his hand to ensnare his sword. The technique for the third guard, on folio 71r, involves thrusting high and around his neck, taking the foe off his horse.

Folios 71v and 72r are a pair of mounted wrestling techniques which appear regularly in images, verse, and glosses of the various Liechtenauer tradition sources. The first is a counter technique for when your opponent tries to seize your neck while riding beside you; the remedy is to apply either a lock to the attacking arm or wrench him by his helmet, applying the original version of the *Sonnen Zaigen*, or "Sun Pointer," adapted to the messer and longsword earlier in this manuscript.

The second wrestling technique is another tried and true method from German *Fechtbücher*: the *Schaff Griff*, or "Sheep Grip." Here, the other rider has approached you head on—"under the eyes" as this manuscript and others have it—driving his right arm under your neck in an attempt to 'clothesline' you. In response you pin his

---

[24] "Von Danzig Fechtbuch," Codex 44 A 8, Rome, 1452, ff. 41v – 42r.

arm down against your chest and ride onward. An alternate solution, and the one illustrated in the plate, is to grab hold of his horse's bridle, wrenching the horse's neck and throwing both horse and rider over. Presumably, this second option would have to be performed before the antagonist is able to grab one's neck. This option is also a regular part of the mounted combat repertoire of sundry fight books.

The final plate of this section, and the manuscript, concludes with more lavish artwork, and describes in general terms what to do when you've forced your opponent off of his mount:

> *If he has been forced off or fallen then dismount also from your horse and work quickly with the wrestling as you well know. If he falls to his back then contain him with a leg with the other on his arm and work with the sword or dagger so that he gives up.*

The image shows one knight constraining his foe on the ground, his sword readied for a killing thrust. In contrast to the simple renderings of full and partial armours in the rest of the equestrian segment, some detail is given to the late 15th-century Gothic plate armours worn by both combatants. This interesting, and higher quality, artwork is a fitting conclusion to Falkner's manuscript.

Related Manuscripts

Peter Falkner's work may have influenced several other works. I choose the word 'may' because there is always the possibility that these manuscripts may have drawn upon a source that Falkner in turn utilized himself; we cannot be sure without further evidence from the 'fossil record'.

Manuscript Cl. 23842[25] in Paris' Cluny Museum certainly appears related to Falkner's *Fechtbuch*. The artwork is very similar, so much so that one is tempted to believe it the product of the same artist, or at least the same workshop. Alas, at this writing, I have had access to but a small subset of this large manuscript's images—35 out of the over 300 that make up this sparsely-captioned, illustrated manuscript. Even out of this small number, four images bear startling resemblance to those in Falkner. Folios 140r and 140v look like Falkner's 2nd and 3rd mounted sword guard images. Folio 181 of the Cluny manuscript shows the same forlorn defense against the dueling shield using only the dagger, and folio 189r has the same poleaxe technique as Peter Falkner has on folio 63v.

The Cluny manuscript includes a number of combat forms not seen in Falkner. Among these are the spear on foot, sword and buckler, wrestling, a man vs. woman duel, armoured foot combat with the half-sword, and the use of what appears to

---

[25] Formerly Codex 862 from Castle Donaueschingen.

be a long-handled mace or *Godendac*—a form of staff weapon associated with the lowland countries. Could this be a copy of Falkner, expanded in scope, but unfinished for its paucity of text? Again, without more data, we may only speculate.

As noted above, Jörg Wilhalm's manuscripts may show some signs of influence from Falkner. While the artwork is far different, the similarity in depictions of the Schielhau and the Sprechfenster is compelling. Interesting too are the similarities between the armoured foot combat of the Cluny manuscript and Wilhalm's treatment of that subject, suggesting further connection between this potential 'family' of manuscripts.

MASTER PETER FALKNER'S
ART OF KNIGHTLY DEFENSE
KK5012

Transcribed by
Dierk Hagedorn and Christian Henry Tobler

Translated by
Christian Henry Tobler

with editorial assistance from
Dr. Jeffrey Forgeng and Dierk Hagedorn

Cover

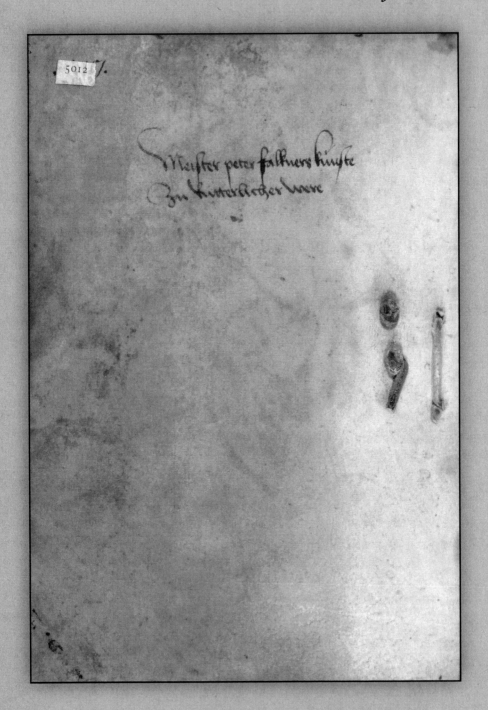

Inside front cover

Meister peter falkners kunste
zu Ritterlicher Were

Master Peter Falkner's Art
of Knightly Defense

End sheet obverse

II 124 D [later hand]

End sheet obverse

Blank

1r

Blank

Junst Ritter lern gott lieb haben, vnd frawen
Eueren, Vnnd red den leytten wol
Biß manlich wa man sol, Do wertist dein er
vber ritterschaft Vnd lern kunst die dich
Jert jn krieg zu eren hoffiert

Recht herr lern
von der rechten hand geru,
vander die were
Die wir an ajuster geloben
Fur kunsten zeloneum

Oberhaw

Zcornhaw

kraumphaw.

Swerchhaw

Schilhaw

Schaittelhaw

1v • *Longsword* (ff. 1v–18r)

Jungk Ritter Lern gott lieb haben / und frawen
In eren / Vnnd red den leytten wol
Biß manlich wā man sol So wechst dein er
vber ritterschaft Vnd lern kunst die dich
ziert In krieg zu eren hoffiert

Sechs hew lern
Von der rechten hand gern
Wider die were
Die wir maister geloben
In künsten zelonenn

Oberhaw
Zornhaw
Krumpphaw
Zwirchhaw
Schilherhaw
Schaittelhaw

Young knight learn to love God, women
revere and the speech that leads well
Be manful when you should be so your honor increases
Practice knighthood and learn the art
that adorns you and honors you in war.

Six strokes learn
from the right hand
against the opposition
which we masters promise
in your art you will be rewarded

Above Stroke
Wrath Stroke
Crooked Stroke
Thwart Stroke
Squinting Stroke
Scalp Stroke

Merck was ich dir sag / Ain oberhaw recht schlag /
Vnnd lingk gegen rechtem / Starck soltu Fechten
Auch magstu dar Inen hengen vnd Zu stichen pringe~

Mark what I say to you: a stroke from above strike true
And left against right should you strongly fight
Also you can therein hang, and the thrust bring

2r

Merck was ich die styck i pin oberhaw recht schlag
Vnd kuist ytezen derytem Sterck soltu fechten
Auch machsten dar men heryten und zu stechen prueste

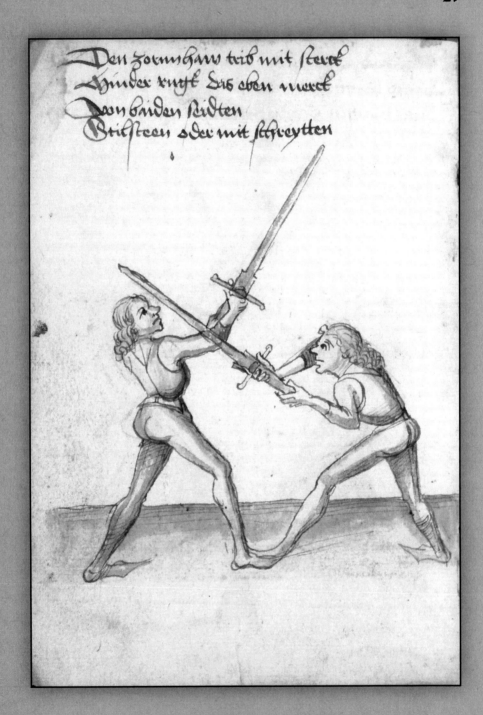

Den zorenhaw trib mit sterck
Hinder ruck das eben merck
Von baiden siditen
Stildten oder mit streytten

2v

Den zornnhaw trib mit sterck
Hinder rugk das eben merck
Von baiden seidten
Stilsteen oder mit schreytten

The Wrath Stroke do with strength
Backward jerk, this also mark
From both sides
Standing still, or with strides

In zornnortt thu° recht winden
Wilt Im das antlit ploß finden
Wirt er sein gewar
So nym es oben ab onefar /
Haw stich merck Im b^and waich od~ hert

With the Point of Wrath do truly wind
If his face's opening you want to find
If of that he becomes aware
Then take off above without fear
Strike, thrust, note in the bind, soft or hard

3r

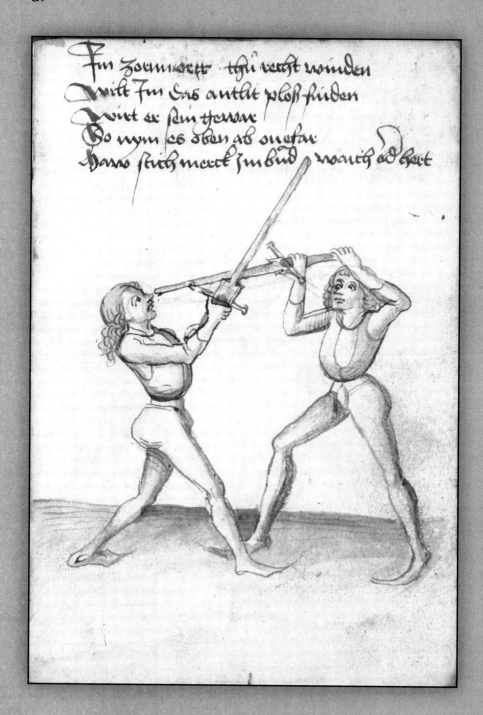

Indes ver ynd nach
An huetten sey dw nit gnach
wer sich des kriegs remet
Ober indas remit er besthemet
In allem winden/Haus stich sich lertt
            2 finden

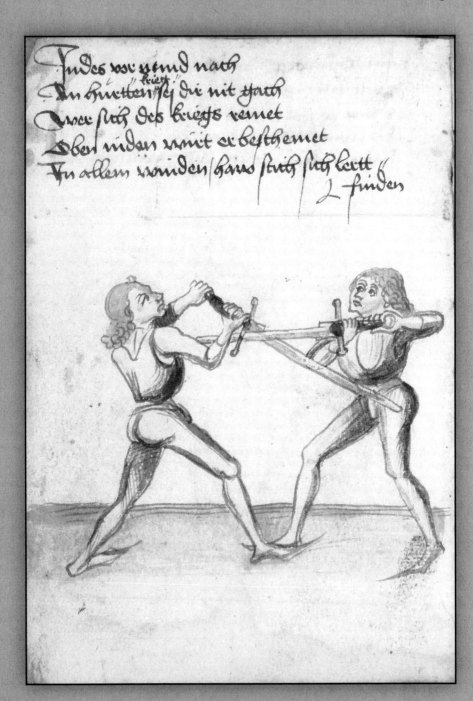

3v

Indes vor vnnd nach
An hurtten krieg sej dir nit gach
Wer sich des kriegs remet
Oben niden wirt er beschemet
In allem winden / haw stich sich lertt finden

Instantly, Before and After
Your war should not be in haste
Who tends to the war
above, is shamed below
In all winding, strike, thrust, these learn to find

Vier bleß lern schlahen vnd prechen
Wiltu dich rechen
Obnan doppellirn / vnd vndan recht mutirn
Ich sag für war
Sich schutzt kain man onefar

Four openings strike and break
if you want to avenge yourself
Above double and below transmute
I say to you truthfully:
no one defends himself without danger

4r

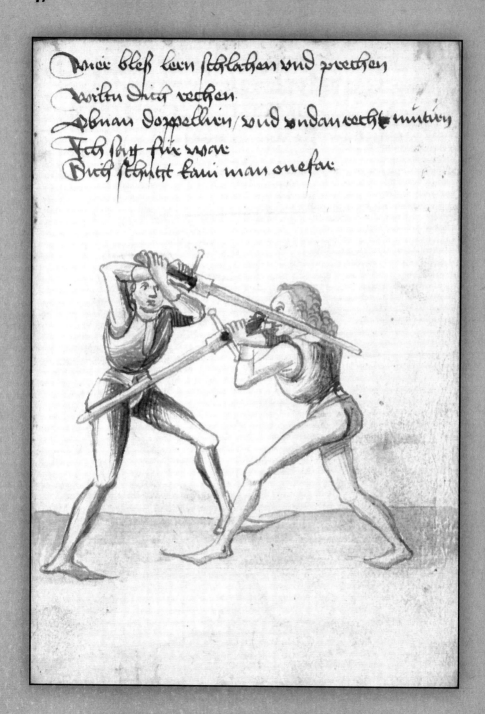

krumpp auff behend / wirfft den ort auf die hend
wer wol versetzet / mit schreiten er vil hew
Dann so gleist oben   J letzt
So stand ab das wil ich loben

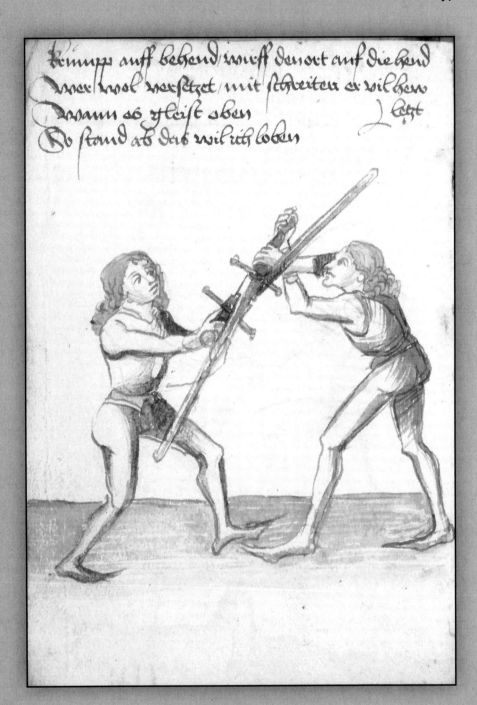

4v

Krumpp auff behend / wirff den ort auf die hend
Wer wol versetzet / mit schreiten er vil hew letzt
Wann es gleist oben
So stand ab das wil ich loben

Strike crooked to him with nimbleness, throw the point on the hands
Who parries well, with stepping he hinders many a stroke
When it clashes above,
Then move away, that I will praise

Die zwirch benympt was vonn oben
darkompt / Oder mit der sterck /
Dein arbait damit merck

The Thwart Stroke takes whatever from above
there comes or with the strong
note your work with this

5r

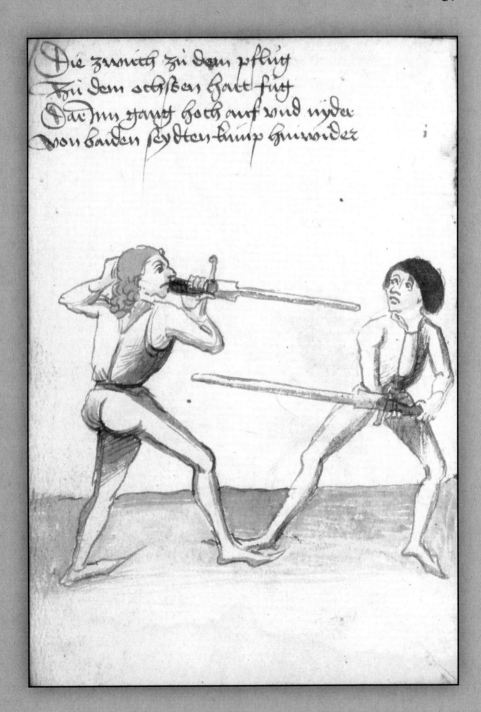

Die zumitth zu dem pflug
Fri dem schitten haut fuir
Dar inn hawt hoch auf und nyder
von baiden sytten lump hinwider

5v

Die zwirch zu dem pflug
Zu dem ochssen hart fug
Dar Inn gang hoch auf und nÿder
Von baiden seydten kump hinwider

The Thwart to the Plow
to the Ochs hard together
Therewith go high up and down
from both sides come again

Die zwirch mit springen
Zu dem haubt laß dir gelingen
Schlach Im zu° baiden oren
So magst auß Im ain rechten doren

The Thwart with springing
to the head let yourself succeed
Strike him to both ears
so you make him a real fool

6r

Die zwerch mit zwerchen
Zu dem haubt laß dir zelnirzen
Schlach im zu banden oben
So nymbst auß im ain rechten boren

6v

Wellicher ain feler recht füret
Nach wunsch errüret
Verker die wing
Durch lauff damit ring

Whoever rightly conducts the failer
Hits at will
The Reverser forces
A running through brings wrestling

Schilher pricht Was biffel schlecht vnd sticht
Schilh zu dem ort
Nym den hals one forcht

The Squinter breaks what a buffalo strikes or thrusts
Squint to the point
Take the throat without fear

7r

Der schnittler ist dem haupt gefer
Den hals und arm durch mit dreyen dritten
Vier stanch mach von baiden seydten

7v

Der schaittler ist dem haupt gefer
Den haw vndan durch mit dreyen driten
Vier straich mach von baiden seydten

The Scalper is a danger to the head
Then strike it through below with three steps
Four strikes make from both sides

Vier leger allain
Dauon halt vnd fluich die gemain
Vier sind der versetzen
Die / die vier leger ser letzen

Four guards alone
these hold and disdain the common
Four are the oppositions
that hurt the four guards very much

8r

8v

Nachraisen lere
Haw stich zwifach ~~td~~ /
damit sere
Stich zu der prust / So gibt es dir lüst /

Learn the traveling after
Strike and thrust twice
and with that trouble
Thrust to the chest, so it gives you delight

Im vberlauffen /
Wind vnd erhöch den knaüffen
Wiltu ringen oder drücken
Die wer soltu zücken /

Overrun him
Wind and go up with the pommel
If you want to wrestle or press
you should grasp the weapon

9r

Jm oberlauffen /
Wmd wud schoth das knauffen
wiltu ruxffen oder druxken
Die wer shtu zucken /

9v

Du solt ansetzen An vier enden In letzen
Er kům oben oder vndan
Ortt geratt ist In verwinden

You should set upon four openings
Whether he comes from above or below
A straight point means to wound him

10r

Ob er starck ist
Durch lauff zů aller frist
Merck die art vnd ler
von baiden seÿdten haw ser

If he is strong
run through in time
Note the way and learn
from both sides powerful strokes

10r

Absetzen lere / haw stich kunstlich were
von vier enden /
haw stich schnidt ler werden

10v

Absetzen lere / haw stich künstlich were
Von vier enden /
Haw stich schnidt ler wenden

Learn to set aside; strike, thrust, artfully defend
From four ends
Strike, thrust and slice learn to apply

Vier sind der schnidt
Zwen oben zwen vnden / mit
Schneidt wider die hertt
Von vndan In baiden gefertt

Four are the slices
Two above and two below
Slice against the hard ones
from below and in both attacks

1r

11v

Schneid wider die kron
von vndan von oban prichstu si schon
Will er an sich reissen
Den knopff oder ortt In das gesicht weisen

Slice against the Crown
from under and from above you break it surely
If he wants to wrench it back
bring the pommel or point to the face

Zucken vnnd dreffen
Den maister wiltu effen
Dridt nachend zŭ dem binden
Das zŭcken geit gŭtt finden

Pull and hit
if you want to fool the master
Step close in binding
The pulling provides good finds

12r

12v

Sprechfenster mach
Stand frölich besich sein sach
Merck was ich sag
Schlag zů Im das es schnab

Do the speaking window
Stand freely and look at his actions
Mark what I say:
Strike to him so that he staggers

Lingk ler arm beschliessen
Halt In vast zůuerdriessen
Beschlossen so er dich hatt
Mitt drucken machstu In madt

Learn to lock the arm on the left
hold him fast to annoy him
If he has you in this way locked
with pressing you weaken him

13r

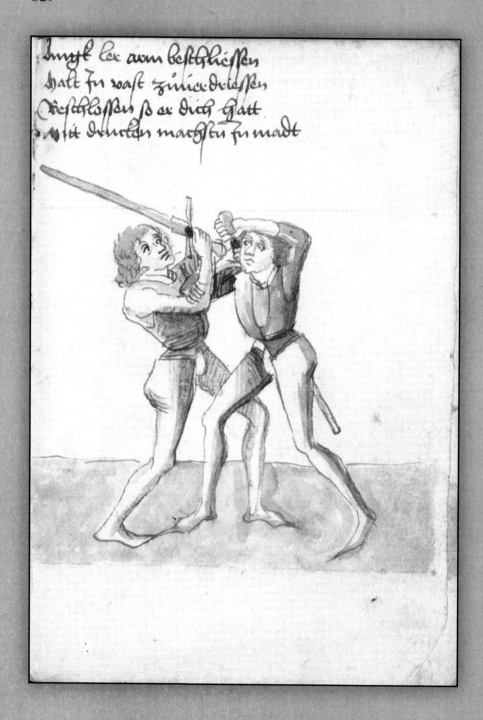

Will er sich retten
Jus fechten entsprechen
Last er die Hand faren
Denck fast gesten den oven

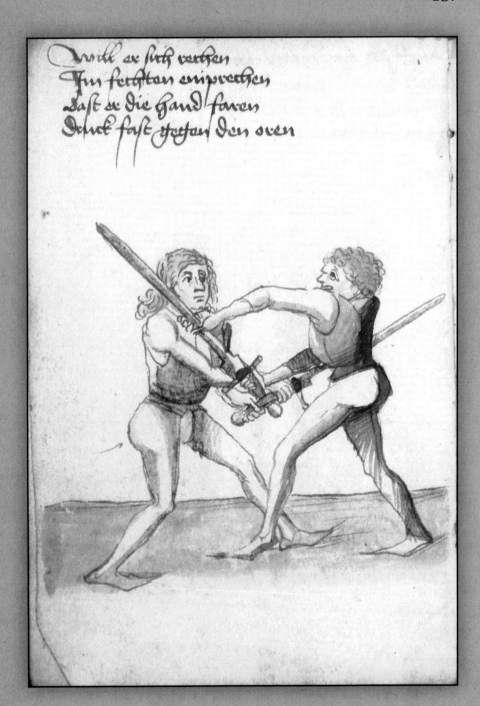

13v

Will er sich rechen
Im fechten einprechen
Last er die hand faren
Druck fast gegen den oren

Whoever wants to avenge himself
and in fighting advance forcefully
If he releases the hand
then press hard against the ear

14r

Lingk vberfar
Rugk gegen bauch wend
Durch baide pain stich behend

Drive over on the left
Turn the back to the belly
Through both legs thrust nimbly

14r

Lunzt wberfar
Durch ytzfas bauth wend
Durch baude pain stich behend

Das Pomm[...] Zayfar,
[...] dem [...] wilt [...] nayſar
[...]witethen
Druck [...] nach [...] dich [...]

14v

Das Sonnen zaigen
Mit dem swert wilt Im naigen
Im einprechen
Druck gegen nack wiltů dich rechen

The Sun Pointer
will bend him with the sword
While advancing forcefully
press against the neck if you want to avenge yourself

Will er dir nahen
Die recht mit ling ler fahen
Setz an die kel oder prust
Gewappnet es gibt dir lŭst

If he wants to come near you
learn to catch the right with the left
Set upon the throat or the chest
The "armed hand"[26] gives you pleasure

---

[26] *Gewappnet* is a word used to describe holding a weapon with one hand on its grip and the other holding the blade, as with the half-sword; i.e., "armoured" combat.

15r

15v

Wiltu In beschemen
Das swert bj dem kiltz nemen
Mitt dem krertz soltu schieben
Mitt baiden henden dich üben

If you want to shame him
take the sword by the hilt
With the cross you should push
with both hands you should endeavor

Auswendig vber durch stechen
Gewappnet ler wer ansprechen
Auch magstu arm beschliessen
Will glick des kanst gewÿessenn

Thrust outside over and through
Learn with the "armed hand" to address the weapon
Also you can lock the arm
if you want to be certain to succeed

16r

16v

Ligt er Indem hangenden ortt
Nym das swert one forchtt
Mitt dem kiltz soltu schieben
Vber rugk dich vben

If he lies in the Hanging Point
take the sword without fear
You should push with the hilt
over the back; this you should endeavor

Wiltu dich vberfalens masen
Hals fach uberbain ler stossen
Arbait schnel biß besumen[?]
Zu stucken mag er hart komen

If you want to refrain from falling over
catch the neck and learn to push over the leg
Work quickly, be mindful:
He can hardly come to his own techniques

17r

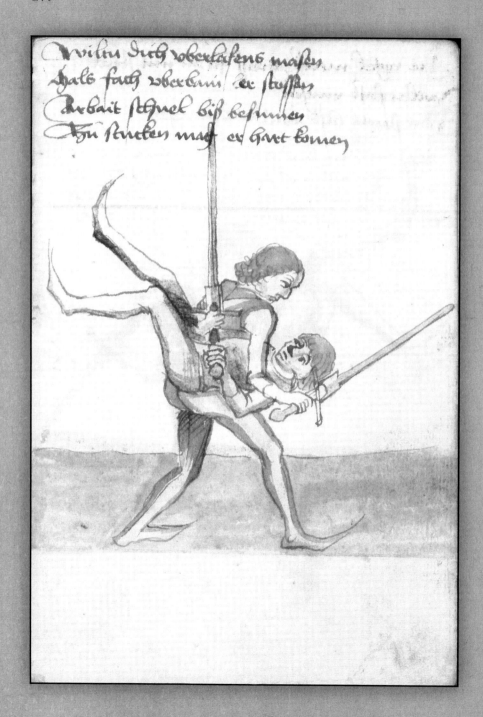

Wiltu dich oberlasens, maßen
halt fach oberhin der stossen
Arbait schnel biß besinnen
zu stücken mag er hart komen

17v

Die regel merck / greiff In an mit sterck /
Wiltu fast ringen
Dein swert lass von dir springen

Mark this rule, attack him with strength
If you are about to wrestle
Let your sword spring from you

Das ist beschliessung der gantzen kŭnst
Wer wol sicht unnd entlichen prichtt
Das best entlichen In drey finden
Wer recht wol henget und winden
damit pringet / Wart mit rechtem leger
betragt / Vnd ir ein winden acht
Winden sind zŭ baiden seÿdten Vnnd
brief die gefert nichtmer waich oder hert

    Hie enndet Maister Peter Falkners
    kunst mit dem langen swertt

This is the conclusion of the complete art
Who observes well and finally breaks
the best surely in three finds
Who hangs properly and the winding
thereby executes; Beware to get along with the correct position
and the appropriated winding; There are eight
windings on both sides and
test the bind no more than soft or hard.

    Here ends Master Peter Falkner's
    art with the longsword

18r

Das ist die beschliessung der gantzen kunst
Wer wol sicht und entlichen prichtt
Das best entlichen in drey finden/
Wer verst wol haimtet und winden
damit preusset/ wart mit rechtem leter
betrafft/ und ie ein der winden acht
winden sind zu baiden seydten und
bieff die gelert michtwer wauch oder heer

Hie enndet Maister Peter Falkners
kunst mit dem langen swertt

Ob du wildt achten
messer fechten betrachten
Ob kein kunst die dich ziert
Zu schimpff vnd zu ernst hofiert

Dehs haw lere

Auß euer hannd wider die were
Die linck hand leg auf den rucken
Auff die prust wilt euer zucken

Zorn haw mercker

Krumtist haw zwinger
Zefer haw mit winckel

18v • Messer (ff. 18v–44r)

Ob du wildt achten
Messer fechten betrachten
So lern kunst die dich ziert
Zu schimpff vnd zu ernst hofiert

Sechs hew lere
Auß ainer hannd wider die were
Die Lingk hand leg auf den rugken
Auff die prust wilt wer zucken

Zorn haw wecker
Enntrist haw zwinger
Gefer haw mit wincker

If you are eager
to strive for messer fighting
then learn the art that adorns you
in play and in earnest combat

Six strokes learn
from one side against the opposition
The left hand place on the back
To the breast if you want to jerk the weapon

Wrath Stroke, Waker
Disarming Stroke, Constrainer
Danger Stroke, with Winker

Was auff dich wirt gericht
Zornhaw ortt das gar bericht
Wiltu In beschemen
Ain messer lern abnemen
Haw stich merck
Im pund waich oder hert /

Whatever is directed to you
The point of the Wrath Stroke breaks this certainly
If you want to shame him
A messer learn to take away
Strike, thrust, note
in the bind, soft or hard

19r

vor vnd nach Indes hab acht
Die lauff des kriegs verht betracht
Den krieg auff les
Oder nyden. wart der ploß

19v

vor vnnd nach Indes hab acht
Die lauff des kriegs recht betracht
Den krieg auff les
Oban nyden wart der pleß

Mind the Before and After, and Instantly
The approach to the War rightly consider
Go on to the War
above, below tend to the openings

Vier sind der zÿnen
Die du solt gewynnen
Der wach nym war
Wa sy seyen mit gefar

Four are the targets
that you should win
Beware of the watch
wherever they pose a threat

20r

Den werffer treib mit sein gefert
Wiß manlich starck vnd hertt
Vñd [~~fluct~~] braich nÿn war
Den hels nÿn auefar

20v

Den wecker treib mit senn gefert
Biß manlich starck und hertt
Der swech nÿm war
Den hals nÿm onefar

The Waker do with its binds
Be manful, strong and hard
Note the weak,
the throat take without fear

Entrist haw nympt was oben darkumpt
Rist zŭ der Sterck
Dein arbait damit merck

The Disarming Stroke takes what comes from above
Get ready in the strong
Your work with it note

21r

Feler verficrt
Die zwen nach erirret
Ob Du verfelest zwisfach
Die schnidt damit mach

21v

Feler verfieret
Die zynen nach errüret
Ob du verfelest zwifach
Die schnidt damit mach

The Failer deceives
to attack the targets
If you miss twice
make the slices with it

Der zwinger In bricht
So der Biffel schlacht vnd sticht
Wer wechsel will trawen
Der zwinger will In berawben

The Constrainer breaks
when the buffalo strikes and thrusts
Who wants to threaten with changing
the Constrainer will rob him of it

22r

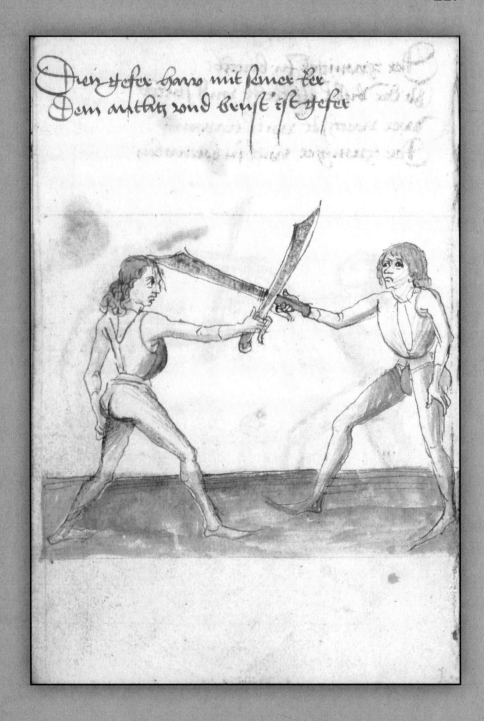

22v

Den gefer haw mit seiner ker
Dem antlitz vnd brust ist gefer

The Danger Stroke with its turn
endangers the face and the breast

23r

Den wincker solt erstrecken
Vnd die Maister damit erwecken
Zwifach ler wincken
Zu der recthen von der lincken

The Winker should stretch forth
and thereby weaken the master
Learn to wink twice
to the right from the left

23r

Wilt die ajaifter zplewen
Des winckers folm dich frewen
was da conzet cannz oder fchlecht
Das fey dem zromeler / allö zerecht

23v

Wilt die masiter plawen
Des winckers soltu dich frewen
Was da kompt krump oder schlecht
Das sei dem wincker alls gerecht

If you want to hit the masters
you should be delighted about the Winker
Whatever comes crooked or straight
these are to the Winker all the same

Vier leger soltu absÿnnen
Inn messer fechten wilen gewÿnen
Pasteÿ Vnd lugißland
Stier vnd eber sei dir bekant /

Four guards should you hold
in messer fighting if you want to be victorious
Bastion and Watchtower
Steer and Boar should be known to you

24r

Wer versetzen solltu beginnen
Das macht du die leser bezwingen
Vor versetzen dich hüt
Versetzen oft den man müt

24v

Vier versetzen Soltu begÿnen
Wiltu die leger bezwingen
Vor versetzen dich hůtt
Versetzen oft den man můt

Four oppositions you should begin
if you want to subdue the guards
Beware of parrying
Parrying is often troublesome

25r

Du solt ansetzen
An vier enden letzen
Er kump oben oder vnden
Ort gerat ist In verwinden

You should set upon
to wound at four targets
Whether he comes above or below
the outstretched point means to wound him

25r

Du folt anfetzen
Jn vier enden letzen
Se krump oben oder vnden
Det gefat ift Zu verwinden

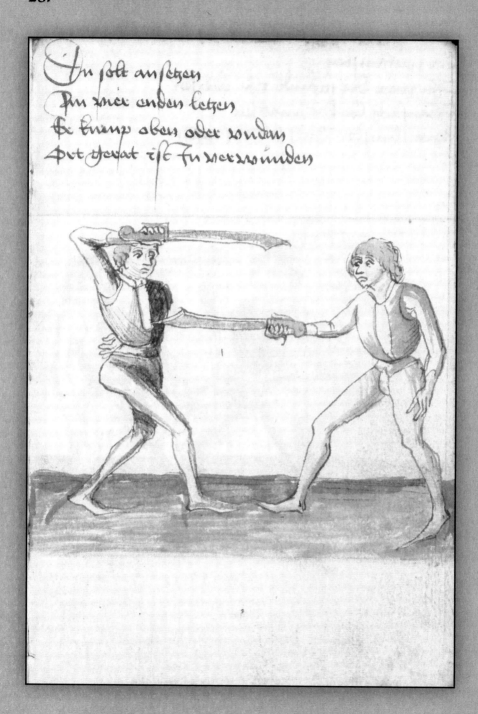

Der nachraissen
Tu mer die schnidt tu weisen
Twifach lex die machen
mit kunsten dich solt besachen

25v

Ler nachraissen
Zu weer die schn^eidt thŭ weisen
Zwifach ler die machen
Mitt künsten dich solt besachen

Learn the traveling after
Know to slice to the weapon
Learn to do this twice
with skill you should perform this

~~Entrist In vberlauff~~
~~Wind vnd erh~~
Vberlauff die vnderram
Sterck vnd In bescham
Ist die versatzung darpracht
Ortt wind kŭrtz biß bedacht

Overrun the lower targets
strongly and shame him
If the parry is done,
wind the point short; be mindful

26r

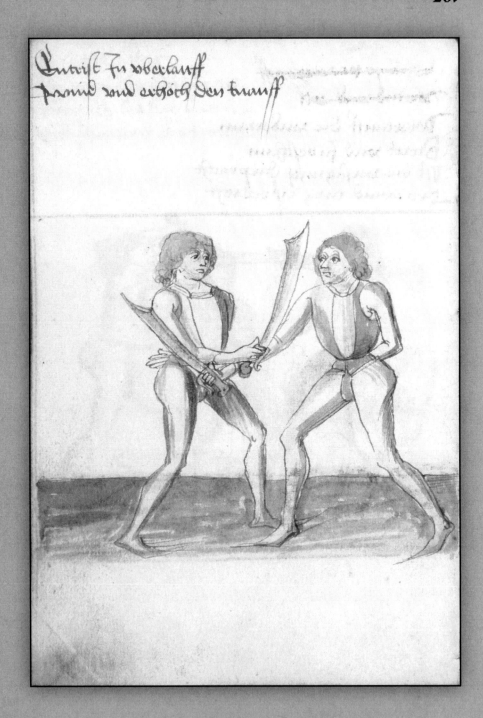

26v

Entrist In vberlauff
Wind vnd erhöch den knauff

With the Disarming [Stroke] overrun
Wind and lift the pommel

Wiltu dich vberlauffens massen
Hals fach vberpain ler stossen

If you want to refrain from overrunning
catch the neck and learn to push over the leg

27r

Zwerchhaw mend
Schwerd mit ort biß behend
will er richten vnd deutten
Stoß ring roer lee zirten

27v

Dein schneid wend
Schneid mit ort biß behend
Will er ringen vnd drücken
Stoß ringe wer ler zücken

Turn your edge
and nimbly slice with the point
If he wants to wrestle and press
push, wrestle, learn to pull the weapon

Die absetzen ler
Haw stich kunstliche wer
Von vier enden
Haw stich ler wenden

Learn the setting aside
to defend stroke and thrust
From four directions
learn to turn [away] stroke and thrust

28r

Durch wechsel das stuck
Die mayster treib zuruckt
Mcrck die art und lee
voon bawden seyttens stich mit feer

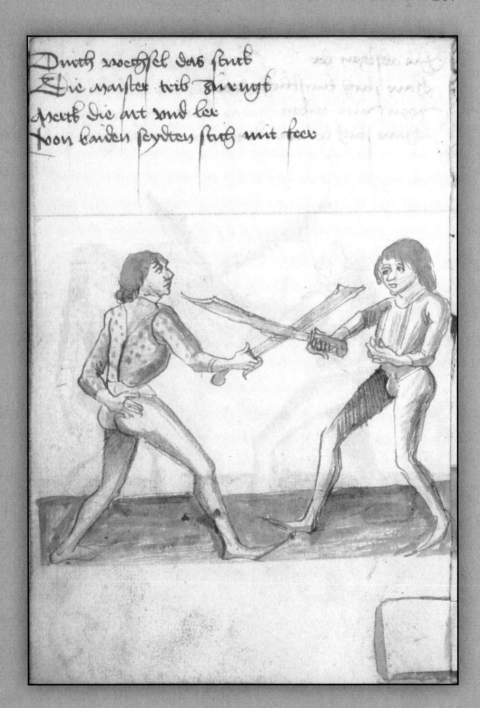

28v

Durch wechsel das stuck
Die maister treib zŭrugk
Merck die art und ler
Von baiden seydten stich mit seer

Changing through, with this technique
repel the masters
Note this method and learn
from both sides to thrust with intent

Wiltu dich Langk vnderhawen
Durch wichsel soltu dich freen
Lingk lanng laß recht ein schiessen
Wind stich wirt In verdriessen

If you want to strike from below long
In the changing through you should rejoice
[from the] left let it shoot forth long
Winding and thrusting are therein vexed

29r

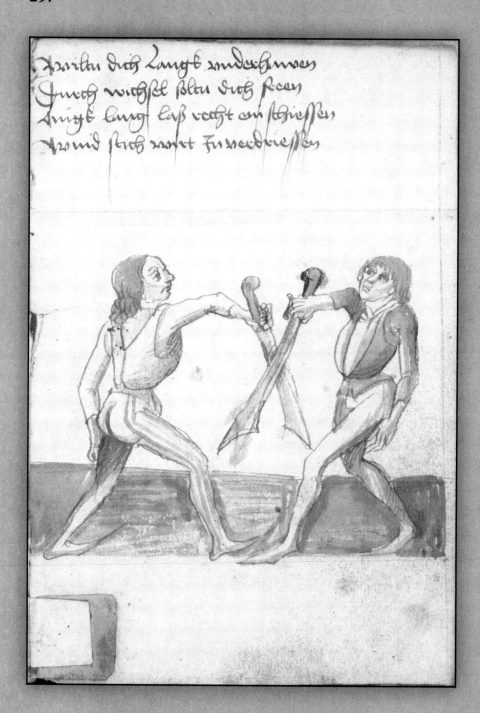

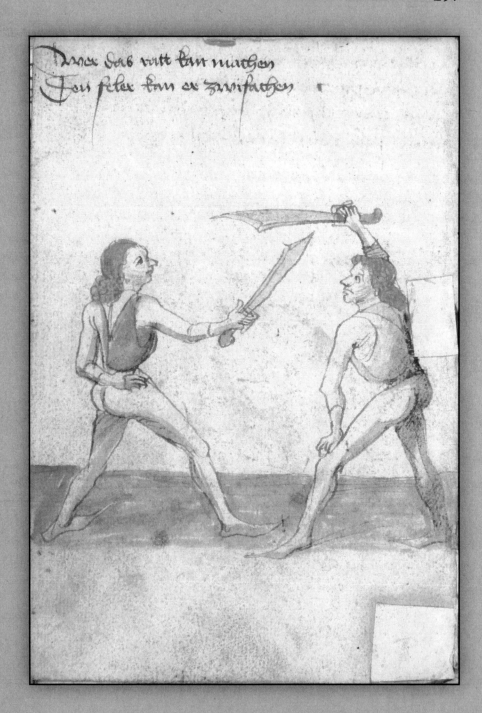

29v

Wer das ratt kan machen
Den feler kan er zwifachen

He who can perform the Wheel
can make the Failer twice

Zuck die treffen
Die maister wiltu effenn
Will er auff dich binden
Zuck schnell will er In finden

Pull from the meeting
if you want to fool the masters
If he wants to bind to you
Pull quickly and you will find him

30r

Haw die flech zum kryeistand
Durch zuck den ortt zehand
Hatt er den stich verletzt
Fedes fel zwoifach er wirt geletzt

30v

Haw die flech zum lugisland
Durch zuck den ortt zehand
Hatt er den stich versetz
Indes fel zwifach er wirt geletzt

Strike the flat to the Watchtower
Pull through the point immediately[27]
If he parries the thrust
instantly feint twice to hinder him

---

[27] The word *zehand* is a synonym for *indes*.

31r

Ob er starck ist
Durch lauff zu allen frist
Der hand unnd arm soltu nahen
Und weislich wartens fahen
Der gelider soltu gewar nemen
Der knie bug soltu dich beremen

If he is strong
Run through always
The hand and arm you should approach
and cleverly attend to grasp
The arms you should truly take
The bend of the knee you should tend

31r

Durch lauff entrist
Den stenbott reib hand zepruff
Nym er das gewicht
Ronder nym macht zenicht

31v

Durch lauff entrist
Den elenbog reib hand zeprust
Nym er das gewicht
Wider nym macht zenicht

Run through [from the] Disarming [Stroke]
Press the hand past the elbow to the breast
If he unbalances you
do the same to him and foil him

Ler arm uber schiessen
In künstlich den beschliessen
Damit In macht feren
Nötten zŭ lauffen oder recht zŭ rüren

Learn to overpower the arm
to skillfully lock it
With this you can lead him,
force him to run or to move properly[28]

---

[28]   Lecküchner says here *oder nicht zu rüeren*, ("or not move"), that is, the lock forces him to
    stand still.

32r

Der von ober schiessen
Tu kunstlich den beschliessen
Damit tu machst sieren
Trötten zu lauffen oder recht zu viren

Da haund paist zu reyben
Wiltu des wapfenantes griff weiben
Dreng vnd ratt
Der lnigken arm robenstblatt

32v

Ler hannd prüst zu reyben
Wiltu den ungenanten griff treiben
Spring und iag
Den lingken arm uberschlag

Learn to press the hand to the breast
if you want to do the Unnamed Grip
Spring and charge;
strike over the left arm

33r

Fach lingk seinen rechten
Die achsel stoß hinder springen fechten

Catch his right with the left
Push the shoulder behind, spring and fight

33r

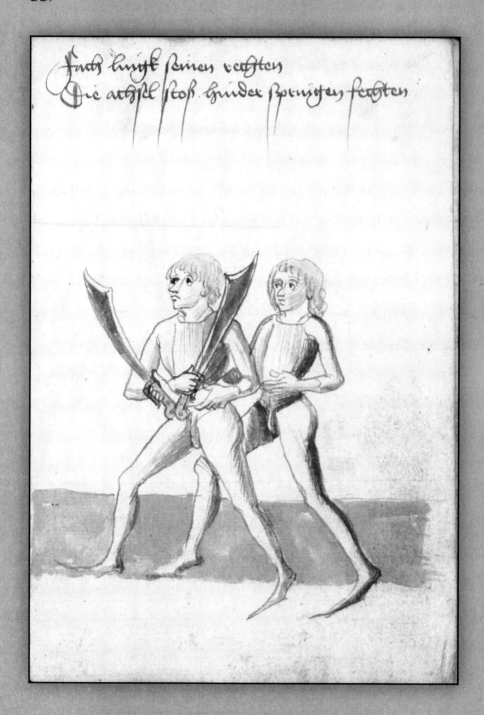

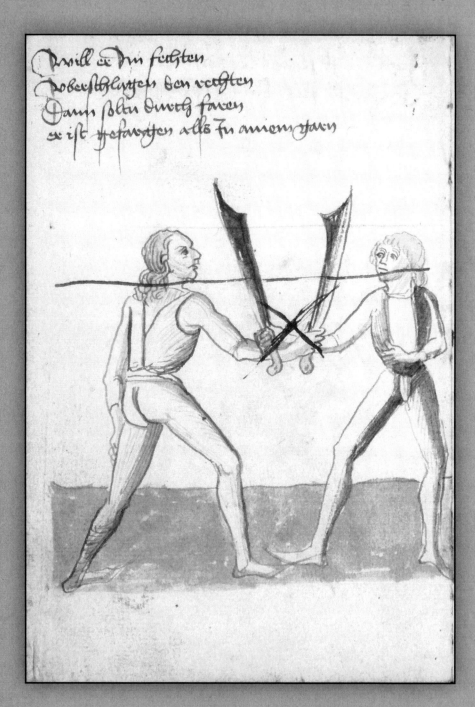

33v

Will er Im fechten
Uberschlagen den rechten
Dann soltu durch faren
er ist gefangen alls In ainem garn

If he wants in the fight
to strike over the right
Then you should drive through
and he is trapped as in a net

Recht mit lingk ler arm beschliessen
Halt In vast zuverdriessen
Beschlossen so er dich hatt
Mitt drucken So er dich macht ~~macht~~ *madt /*

Surely with the left learn to lock the arm
Hold it fast to vex him
If he has you thus locked
he [check]mates you with pressing

34r

Mit verſiß der ſchrindt
Inwen ſundan zwan obcn mitt
Wröll er auß dem band entlos
Die hand ſolt mi dentlen

34v

Nitt vergiss der schnidt
Zwen unden zwen oben mitt
Will er auß dem band rucken
Die hand solt im drücken

Do not forget the slicing
Two below, with two above
If he wants to jerk from the bind
his hand you should press

Das sonen zaigen
Mit dem messer wilt im naygen
Die achsel tasch
Gegen nack druck fast

The Sun Pointer
with the messer will incline him
Slap the shoulder
and against the neck press fast

35r

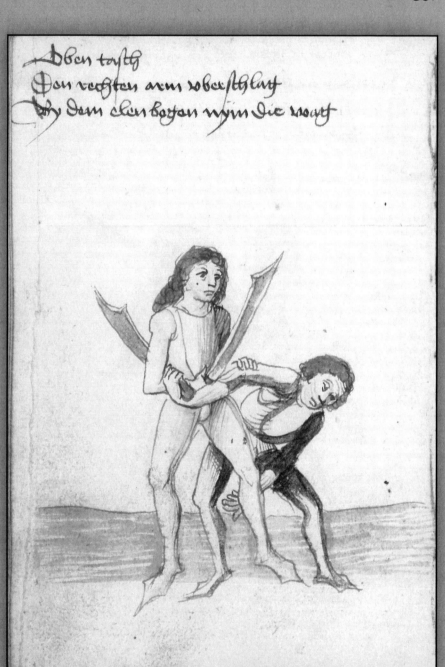

35v

Oben tasch
Den rechten arm uberschlag
By dem elen bogen num die wag

Slap above
The right arm strike over
By the elbow take the balance

Ligt er In hangenden ortt
Nym das messer one forcht
Mitt dem trütz soltu schieben
Mitt baiden schneiden dich üben

If he lies in the Hanging Point
take the messer without fear
With the crossguard you should push
and with both edges you should do this

36r

Wiltu zu kosthemen
Ant lerer hand wer nemer
Tut wechsel ob du will
Die mach hab hinder dem schilt

36v

Wiltu In beschemen
Mitt lerer hand wer nemen
Zuck wechsel ob du wild
Die wach hab hinder dem schilt

If you want to shame him
take the weapon with the empty hand
Pull, change, if you wish
The guard have behind the shield

Im winden biß bericht
Dem ort trift und sein erpricht
Messer nemen solt enperen
Mitt reissen dich zu Im leren

Be prepared in the winding
Your point hit and his breaks
Abandon taking the messer
Learn to turn to him with wrenching

37r

Jm winden biß bericht
Den ort trieff vnd sin ezpricht
Messer nemen solt enparen
Aynt reissen durch zu Jm teren

Den bosses zwisfach
Den arbait damit mach
Was vons bosses lang kumpt
Dett schnell das abnimpt

37v

Den bogen zwifach
Dein arbait damit mach
Was vom bogen lang kumpt
Ortt schnell das abnimpt

The Bow twice
Your work therein do
What comes long from the Bow
the point quickly takes away

Mitt dem messer nemen
Machstu In beschemen
Mitt lerer hand wer nym
Uber wind auff lingk druck geswind

With the messer taking
you make him ashamed
With the empty hand take the weapon
Wind over to press with the left fast

38r

Haſtu am wer
wieſtu vberlauffen mit geſer
ſtich an ſchaden
fauſtu dich tern
Stand frelich machſtu dich woren

38v

Hastu ain wer
Wirstu uberlauffen mit gefer
Ruck an schaden
Kanstu dich lern
Stand frolich machstu dich weren

If you have a weapon
and are overrun with the Danger Stroke
Pull without damage
if you can learn
to stand calmly you can defend yourself

Ob er starck ist
Und stätt in künstlich list
Gewappnet will er wenden
Rück ort thŭt In enden

If he is strong
and stands with skillful sense
The "armed hand" wills him to turn
Wrench the point and put him to an end

39r

39v

Aussen über durch stechen
Gewappnet ler außprechen
Auch machstu arm beschliessen
Will gelück das kanst gewyessen

Thrust outside over and through
Learn to break away with the "armed hand"
Also you can lock the arm
if you want to be sure to succeed

Will er prangen so der arm is gefangen
Arm uberfar In die kel
Mitt drucken soltu nicht felen

If he wants to catch the arm
drive the arm over to the throat
With pressing you should not fail

40r

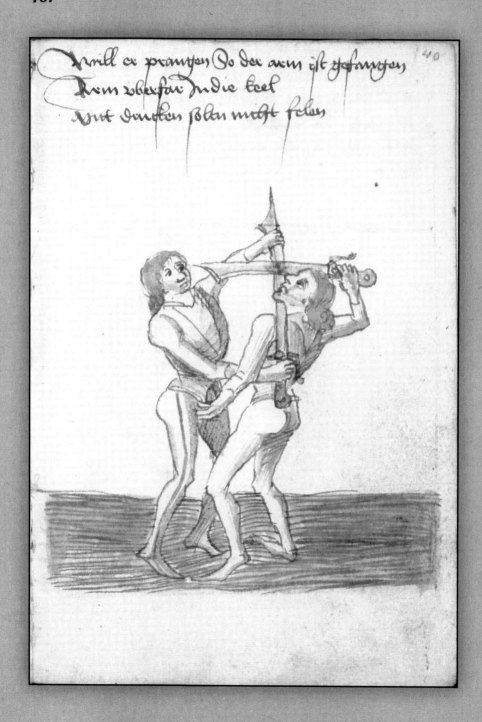

Will er dich besthamen
Das messer bj dem zchilt nemen
Den hand ler ruclen
Den alenbogen foltu druclen

40v

Will er dich beschemen
Das messer bi dem gehiltz nemen
Dem hand ler rucken
Den elenbogen soltu drücken

If he wants to shame you
and take the messer by the hilt
Learn to jerk his hand
the elbow you should press

Auff recht will er wencken[29]
Und arm rencken
Linck hinder ler springen
Die achsel recht soltu dringen

If he wants to dodge high on the right
and twist the arm
Learn to spring behind with the left
The shoulder you should truly press

---

[29]   Lecküchner says "bencken."

41r

Bnvl roberfar
Vnck getzas bamth raxend
Omath bande pais firch bethend

41v

Linck uberfar
Ruck gegen bauch wend
Druch baide pain stich behend

Go over to the left
Turn the back against the belly
Thrust through both legs nimbly

Das messer zů dem rechten bain halt
Die wer bricht mit gewalt
Den lingken foß vor satz
Mitt schreytten haw stich letz

Hold the messer to the right leg
the defense break with force
The left foot set forward
Strike, thrust, and wound with stepping

42r

Das messer zu dem rechten bein halt
Die vor bericht mit gewalt
Den linicken boß vor fatz
mitt schreytten haw stich letz

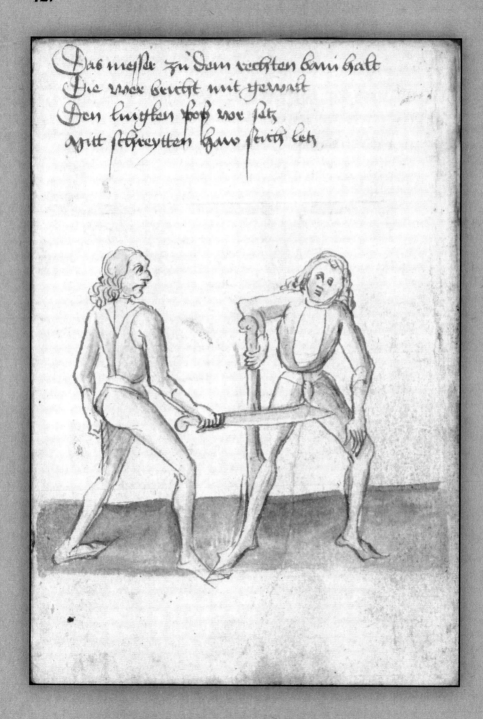

Kurtz dich meld
Fin bind biß schnell
Haw stich zu seiner angsten
Der rechten hand soltu umbken

42v

Kurtz dich meld
In bind biß schnell
Haw stich zu seiner lingken
Der rechten hand soltu wincken

Announce yourself briefly
In the bind be quick
Strike, thrust to his left
you should Wink[30] to his right hand

---

[30]   That is, strike a Winkerhau.

Scorpian mit seinem gefer
Mitt antlitz biß gefer
Die kurtz schneid gegen dem haubt laß fallen
Schlag recht zwifach laß prallen

The Scorpion with its threat
With it the face is endangered
The short edge let fall against the head
Strike surely twice let it bounce

43r

Storpern mit schwerz zhefer
gut antlitz biß zhefer
Die kurtz schwerd zhefen dem haubt laß fallen
Stchlag recht zwerstrich laß prallen

Holt mit seiner wart
In das oren stoft er hartt
In des biß behend
Verwappnet ort zu rosicht wend

Hie endet Maister Peter Fallners kunst
mit dem messer

43v

Klotz mit seiner wart
Zu den oren stost er hartt
In des biß behend
Gewappnet ort zu gesicht wend

Hie enndet Maister Peter Falkners kunst
Mitt dem Messer

The pommel with his defense
thrusts hard to the ear
Instantly be nimble
With the "armed point" turn to the face

Here ends Master Peter Falkner's Art
with the Messer

44r

[Latin] *IHS Nazarenus Rex Iudeorum*

Jesus of Nazareth, King of the Jews

44r

Blank

45r

Blank

45v

Blank

46r • *Dagger* (ff. 46r–56r)

Hye hept sich an das degen fechten
ym harnisch Wiltu das ver-
borgen sey so er felt so reyß yme
große stück von sinem wappenrock
Und stiche yme yn sin vysier mit
dem degen so sichstu das er mit
nichten mag ledig werden das
wer gůt wer es sandig so ge-
wyndt man yme groß vorteyle
abe

Here begins the dagger fighting in harness. If you want this to be secret, then if he falls wrench a large piece from his coat armour and thrust it into his visor with the dagger; thus you see to it that he cannot free himself. This is good when it is sandy, thus one wins a great advantage.

46r

Hye hept sich an das degen fechten
ym harnisch Wiltu das ver
hortzen sey so er felt so reyß yme
grosse stuck von sinem woppenrock
Und stiche yme yn sin vysyer mit
dem dertzen so sichstu das er mit
nichten mag ledig werden das
wer gut wer es sandig so ye
wyndt man yme groß vorteyle
abe

Item sticht er dir oben zů so ver setz ym
mit dem lincken arm vnd mit der zechten
hand stich ym nach den gesicht ver setzt er dir
auch den stich so zock starck an dich sticht er
dan hin vnder so ver setz ich vnd wind den
techer sůz zc

46v

Item sticht er dir oben zů so ver setz ym
mit dem lincken arm und mit der rechten
hand stich ym nach dem gesicht vor setz er dir
auch den stich so röck stark an dich sticht er
dan hin wider so ver setz hoch und nymb den
tegen üß &c

Item, if he thrusts above to you, then parry with the left arm and with the right hand thrust to the face. If he parries your thrust also, then jerk strongly to yourself. If he thrusts again, then parry high and take the dagger from [him] etc.

Item sticht er aber oben zů so fach sin hand in
din hand und mit der andern do der degen in
ist schleg im über sinen rechten arm sines
gleichß und ruck an dich daß heisset ein
degen nemen und ist gut &c

Item, if he thrusts again above, then catch his hand in your hand and with the other, the one holding the dagger, strike over his right arm to his wrist and jerk it to yourself. This is called a dagger taking and is good etc.

47r

Item fart er ein langen stich auff dich so far
mit dinem degen vnden durch an sin hand
vnd mit der lincken hand vorne vmb
den hals vnd wurff in vber das linck
bein das ist gut zu

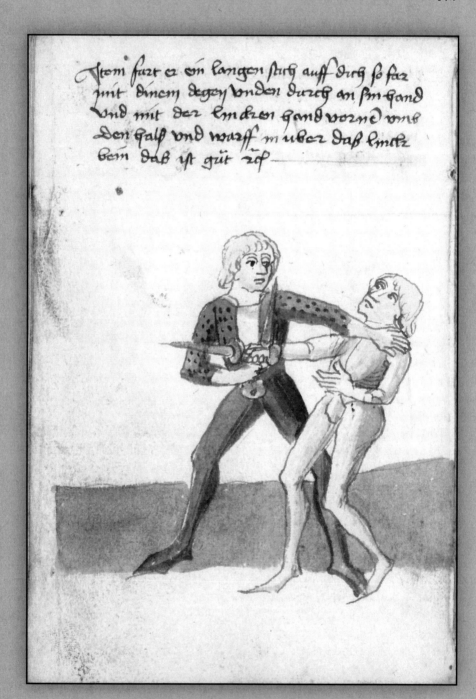

47v

Item furt er ein langen stich auff dich so far
mit dinem degen unden durch an sin hand
und mit der lincken hand vornen umb
Den halß und wurff [i]m uber daß linck
bein daß ist güt &c

Item, if he drives a long thrust to you, then drive with your dagger under through to his hand and with the left hand in front and around his neck and throw him over the left leg. That is good etc.

Item sticht er dir aber oben zů So gryff
mit diner lincken hand in din degen
und ver setz im den stich gewappnet und
wind ym den tegen auß daß heist der ober
schilt daß ist aüch güt &c

Item, if he thrusts again above to you, then grasp with your left hand
to your dagger and parry his thrust "with the armed hand" and wind
his dagger from [him]. That is called the Upper Shield and this is also
good etc.

48r

Item sticht er dir aber oben zu So griff
mit diner lincken hand in din degen
vnd versetz im den stich gewapnet vnd
wind ym den tegen auß das heist der aber
schilt das ist auch gut ꝛc

Item suecht er aber oben zů so veseez ym mit lincker
hand vnd mit der rechten gryff vnden durch sin
rechtes bein vnd mit dem kopff durch sin üchssen
vnd heb da mit vbersich so wirffet du yn nider
das ist mit ledigen henden ꝛc

48v

Item sticht er aher oben zů so verselz ym mit lmkcer
hand und mit der rechten gryff unden durch sin
rechteß bein und mit dem koph durch sin üchsen
und heb da mit ubersich so wurffest du yn nider
daß is mit ledigen henden &c

Item, if he thrusts again above, then parry him with the left hand and with the right grasp under through to his right leg and with the head through [under] his armpit and lift him thereby upward so that you throw him down. This is [performed] with empty hands etc.

Item sticht er dir aber oben zů so leg din tegen
über din lincken arm daß der spitz ubersich
gee und umb schrenck ym sin hand und tegen
Ruck zů den erden daß heissett die scher &c

Item, if he thrusts to you again above then place your dagger over
your left arm so that the point goes upward and enclose his hand and
dagger. Jerk towards the earth; this is called the Scissors etc.

49r

Item sticht er dir aber oben zu° so ver setz mit
dem rechten arm und her weysz ym sin hand mit
der lincken hant seinen rechten elebogen ruck
die under din brust und wurff in uber das
bem das heisst das vngenant ⸻

49v

Item sticht er dir aber oben zŭ so ver setz mit
dem rechten arm und her wisch ym sin hand mit
der lincken hant seinen rechten elebogen ruck
die unden din brust und wurff in uber daß
bein daß heisst daß ungenant

Item, if he thrusts again to you above, then parry with the right arm and catch his hand and with the left hand [catch] his right elbow. Jerk these under your breast and throw him over the leg. This is called the Unnamed.[31]

---

[31] Several different techniques involving the isolation of the opponent's weapon arm are described throughout the manuscripts of the Liechtenauer tradition with the title of "Unnamed."

Item aber ein stück sticht er dir oben zů so leg
din tegen uff den rechten arm daß den spitz hin-
densich stee sticht er dan uff dich so versetz ym den
stich mit dem tegen und griff mit der lincken
hant uber sin recht ym din arm und drück hin-
densich daß heist daß schloß ringen ym tegen

Item, another technique: if he thrusts to you above, then place your dagger on your right arm so that the point faces backward. If he thrusts then to you, then parry his thrust with the dagger and grasp with the left hand over his right arm to your arm and press backward. This is called Lock Wrestling at the dagger.

50r

Item aber ein stück sticht er dir oben zu so leg
dm tegen uff den rechten arm das der spitz übm
désich sté sticht er dan uff dich so verschz ym den
stich mit dem tegen vnd griff mit der lincken
hant über sin recht ym din arm vnd drücke ihm
dersich das geist das schloß ringen ym tegen

Item stiecht er dir vnden zu° so vaß ÿm mit
diner tegen uff den sin vnd mit der lincken
hant begriff ÿm sin recht vnd ruck an dich so
nÿmstu ÿm den tegen vnd stiecht sich selbß
daran das ist gůt

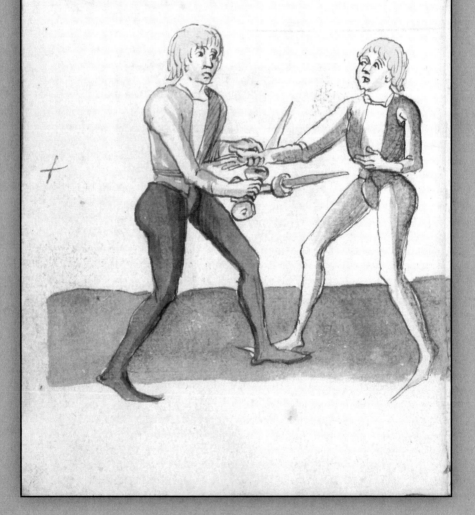

50v

Item slich er dir unden zů so val ym mit
dinem tegen uff den sin und mit der lincken
hand begriff ym sin recht und ruck andich so
  — *nymstu ym den tegen und sticht sich selbß*
da ran daß ist güt

Item, if his thrusts to you below, then fall upon him with your dagger to his. And with the left hand grasp his right [hand] and jerk towards yourself so that you take his dagger and in doing so he thrusts himself with it. That is good.

Item sticht er aber unden zů so val aüch uff den
tegen mit dym und griff mit der lincken hend
in sy beid tegen und mit der rechten wind unden
duch uber sich so nympt ym den tegen daß heist
der under schilt

Item, if he thrusts again below, then fall also upon his dagger with
yours and grasp with the left hand to both daggers. And with the right
wind under and up so that you take his dagger. This is called the Lower
Shield.

51r

Item sticht es aber unden zu so val ym auch uff den
tegen mit dym und griff mit der lincken hend
in sy bed tegen vnd mit der rechten romd vnden
durch uber sich so nymist ym den tegen das heist
der vnder sticht

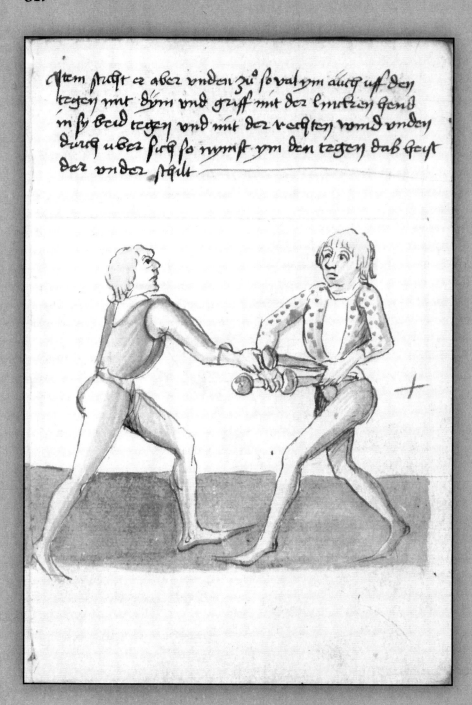

Aber ein gut meisterlich stuck mit dem tegen
hastu ein tegen vnd er kein vnd sticht dir vnden
zu so versetz ym mit diner lincken hand wol uff
sein rechten arm vnd hinder ruck ym die hand
vnd nym ym sin tegen Vnd halt in also fast
oder furtz wo du wilt das herst die uß fu zug

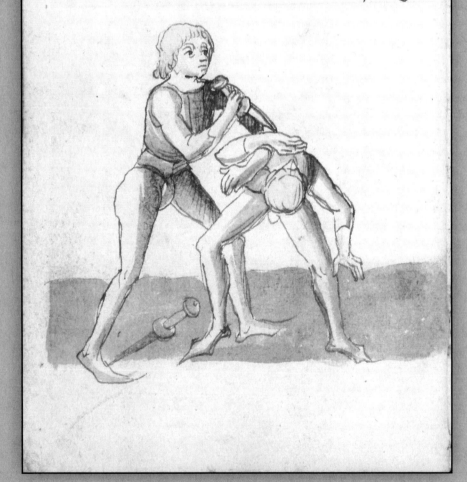

51v

Aber ein güt meisterlich stuck mit dem tegen
Hastu ein tegen und er kein und sticht dir unden
zů so versetz ym mit diner lincken hand wol uff
sein rechten arm und hinder rück ym die hand
und nym sin tegen und halt [i]m also fast
oder fürn wo du wilst daß heist die ußfürug~

Another good masterful technique with the dagger. If you have a dagger and he has none[32] and thrusts to you below, then parry with the left hand well to his right arm and jerk his hand behind him and take his dagger and hold him fast or lead him wherever you wish. This is called the Leading Away.

---

[32] Actually, the technique demands just the opposite: he is armed and you are not. This is clearly a scribal error.

52r

Item aber ein stück hat er ein tegen und du kein
sticht er dan dir unden zů so griff ym mit beiden
henden sein rechte hant und rück die uber din
lincke achsel daß ist ein wurff oder arm bruch

Item, another technique: if he has a dagger and you do not and he thrusts below to you, then grasp his right hand with both hands and jerk it over your left shoulder. This is a throw or an arm break.

52r

Item aber ein stuck hat er ein tegen vnd du kein
stuck er dan dir vnder zu so gruff jm mit beiden
henden sein rechte hant vnd wurtz die vber din
lincke achsel das ist ein wurff oder arm bruch

Item hastu ein tegen vnd er auch ein vnd sticht dir
oben zu̇ über den krafft so wirff dich mit dine
krafft vnden durch in sin prust vnd stich ym
mit dinem tegen hinden vmb sin bein oder
durch sy bein vnd ruck an dich so velt er nider
das ist gut ———————

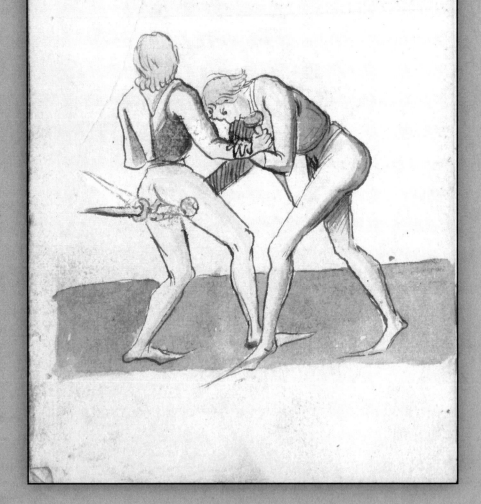

52v

Item hastu ein tegen und er auch ein und sticht dir
oben zů uber den kopff so wurff dich mit dine~
kopff unden durch in sin brust und stich ym
mit ebichen tegen hinden umb sin bein oder
durch sy beid und rück andich so velt er nider
daß ist güt

Item, if you have a dagger and he also has one and thrusts to you above over the head, then throw yourself with your head under and through to his breast and thrust to him with your dagger inverted around behind his leg or through both and jerk toward yourself so that he falls down. That is good.

Item hastu ein tegen und er ein und sticht uff yn
nympt er dir din tegen so entsetz dich ym üß
alß ym schwert sticht er dan uff dich von oben
nider so versetz ym mit der lincken hand und
mit den koph lauff ym durch sin rechten arm
und mit diner rechten hand begrieff ym sin
bein und heb yn ubersich so wurffstu yn

Item, if you have a dagger and he has one and [you] thrust to him and
he takes your dagger, then let yourself be relieved of it, as with the
sword.[33] If he then thrusts to you downward from above, then parry
that with the left hand and run through his right arm with your head,
and with your right hand grab his leg and lift it upward so that you
throw him.

---

[33] Falkner is applying some wisdom common to all weapons use here: if you are about to lose
    your weapon, don't struggle to keep hold of it; just let it go and grapple with the opponent.

53r

Item hastu ein tegen vnd er ein vnd stichst vff yn
nymmpt er dir den tegen so entsetz dich ynuch
als ym schwert sticht er dan vff dich von oben
nider so versetz ym mit der lincken hand vnd
mit dem kopff lauff ym durch sin rechten arm
vnd mit diner rechten hand begruff ym sin
bein vnd heb yn vberstich so wurffstu yn ___

Item aber ein stück sticht er dir oben zu mit dem
tegen so versetz ym mit der lincken hand hoch
vnd mit der rechten schlag ym din tegen vmb
sin hals vnd ruck an dich oder greiff mit der
lincken ym din tegen vnd drucke ym in das
genick

53v

Item aber ein stück sticht er dir oben zů mit dem
tegen so versetz ym mit der lincken hand hoch
und mit der rechten schlag ym din tegen umb
sin halß und ruck andich oder griff mit der
lincken yn din tegen und druck ym in daß
genick

Item, another technique: if he thrusts above to you with the dagger, then parry it with the left hand high and, with the right hand, strike around his neck with your dagger and jerk it toward yourself or grasp with the left hand to your dagger and press him at the neck.

Item sticht er dir oben zů so versetz ym aber mit
der lincken hant hoch und mit dem tegen schlag
ym in sin gelenck deß rechten armß so bric[h]st
ym den arm oder nymst ym den tegen daß ist
güt

Item, if he thrusts to you above then again parry with the left hand
high and with the dagger strike to the joint of his right arm so that you
break the arm or take the dagger. That is good.

54r

Item sticht er dir oben zuo verseez ym aber mit
der lincken hant hoch vnd mit dem rechen schlag
ym in sin gelenck des rechten armß so brist
ym den arm oder nimst ym den rechen das ist
gut

Item aber ein gut stuke yn dem ringen hat er
emer tegen vnd du kein vnd strist der vnden
zu so fall ym mit diner rechten hant uff sin
recht vnd hinder spring yn mit dinem lin
cken fuß vnd mit der rechten hant begriff
yn sin rechtes bein inder linie pug vnd mit
der lincken hant wirff vmb sin wich das
yst gut

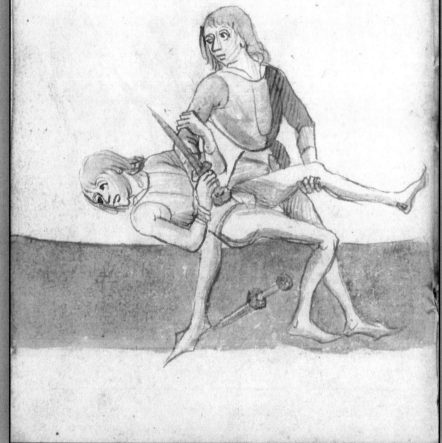

54v

Item aber ein gut stuck yn dem ringen hat er
einen tegen und du kein und sticht dir unden
zů so fall ym mit diner rechten hant uff sin
recht und hinder spring yn mit dinem lin-
cken fuß und mit der rechten hant begriff
ym sin rechteß bein in der knie pug und mit
der lincken hant vornen umb sin waich daß
ost güt

Item, another good technique involving wrestling: if he has a dagger, and you do not, and he thrusts below to you, then fall upon his right hand with yours, and spring behind him with your left foot, and with the right hand, grasp his right leg behind the knee, and with the left hand around the front of his waist. That is good.[34]

---

[34] The text and illustration are in disagreement here: they describe the action on opposite sides of the body. Preliminary practice with this technique points to the illustration being in error.

Item aber ain stück hat er einen tegen und du
keinen sticht er dan uff dich so versetz ym mit
der lincken hand und mit der rechten griff
ym unden an sin ellebogen ruck an dich daß
ist auch güt

Item, another technique: if he has a dagger and you have none and he
thrusts then to you, then parry with the left hand and with the right
grasp below to his elbow and jerk that toward you. That is also good.

55r

Item aber ein stuck hat er einen tegen und du,
kremen stichst er dan uff dich so versetz im mit
der linckey hand und mit der rechten grif
im unden an sin ellebogen ruck an dich das
ist auch gut

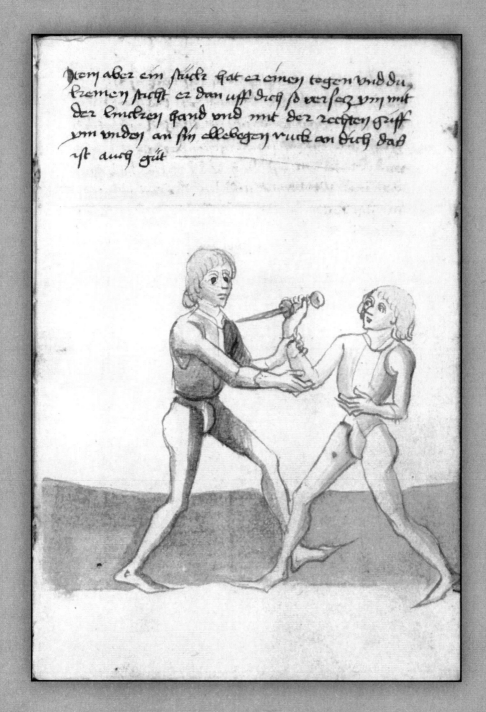

Aber ein stucke halt einer ij tegen im
beiden henden vnd wilt yn tragen wo
du wilt das er dich nit mag stechen so
greiff ym durch sin arm hinderwert legen
vnd druck yn vff den hals mit beiden hen
den vnd heb damit vberstich so kan er dich
nit stechen

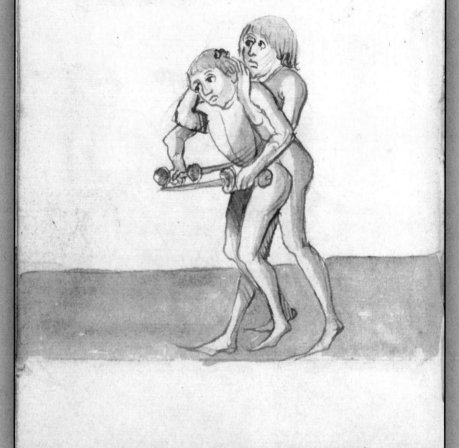

55v

Aber ein stuck hatt einer ij tegen in
beiden henden und wilt yn tragen wo
du wilt daß er dich nit mag stechen so
griff ym durch sin arm hinderwert ligen
und druck yn uff den halß mit beiden hen-
den und heb damit ubersich so kan er dich
nit stechen

Another technique: if one has two daggers, one in each hand, and you
want to lead him wherever you wish so that he cannot thrust to you,
then grasp through his arms while being behind him and press him
on the neck with both hands and lift him thereby upward so that he
cannot thrust to you.

Item aber ein stück hastu ein tegen und er
auch ein sticht er dan uff dich so versetz ym
den stich und nym ym den tegen wart er den
uff din stich und welt dir auch gern den din
nemen so thů einen fel stich und wurff ynn
nider und fal ym uff den lyb schlecht er dir
den einen fuß umb den halß so heb den andern
fest und arbeit ym zů dem gesicht mit dem
tegen daß ist güt

Item, another technique: if you have a dagger and he has one too and thrusts then to you, then parry the thrust and take the dagger. If he defends against your thrust and wants to also then take your dagger, then pretend to do a 'Failer' thrust and throw him down and fall upon his body. If he extends a foot around the neck, then lift the other quickly and work to his face with the dagger. This is good.

56r

Blank

57r

Blank

57v • Saint Mark (f. 57v) and Staff Fighting (ff. 58r–61r)

Stg marg

Saint Mark

Merck waß ich meld ynn der stangen byß
schnel winden und uff heben
fechten und nyder legen ab stürtzen vergiss nit
fünff hew mach mit über fallen und auß winden
how stich sich auch lertt finden daß ist der text
her nach folgett

Note what I say:
be quick with the staff,
winding and lifting,
fighting and laying down.
Do not forget the plunging down,
also do the five strokes,
with falling over and from the winding,
also learn to find strokes and thrusts.
This is the text that follows.

58r

Merck was ich meld ym ~~sunder~~ der stangen daß
~~ist gut das~~ stnel winden dar vnd uff geben
felten vnd nyder legen ab sturczen vergriff mit
funff gew mach mit vber fallen vnd auß winden
haw stich sich auch leret finden das ist der text
her nach folgett

Wiltu zirtlich machen die iiij anbinden soltu
besachen wen du vor ym ligst yn einem wechssel
hauw vnd er laufft dir mit dem ort von
vnden vff zu der brust so lauff ym dar gegen
auch mit dem ort schlecht er dan oben mit
dem andern ort so schlach auch mit dem andern
dar gegen so mage er dir mit schaden

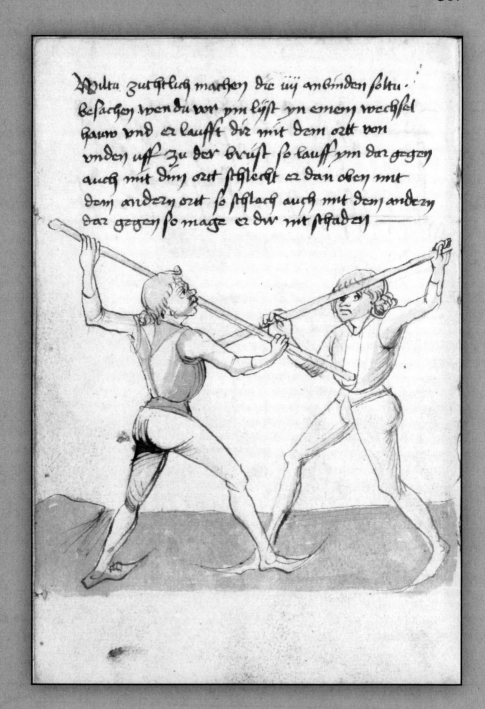

58v

Wiltu zuchtlich machen die iiij anbinden soltu
besachen wen du vor ym lyst yn einen wechsel
hauw und er laufft dir mit dem ortt von
unden uff zu der brust so lauff ym dar gegen
auch mit din ortt schlect er dan oben mit
dem andern ortt so schlach auch mit dem andern
dar gegen so mage er dir nit schaden

"If you want to act with discipline, you should attend to the four bindings." When you lie before him in a Change Stroke and he runs in at you with the point up from below to your chest, then run in against it, also with your point. If he then strikes above with the other point, then strike also with the other against it, so that he cannot harm you.

Aber ein stück daß heist daß über lauffen
wen er dir angebunden hat an die stangen so
fall ym oben uber sin rechte achsel an den halß
mit dem ortt wil er dan den ortt absetzen mit
dem andern ortt der stangen so schlach schnel mit
dinem andern ortt ym zu dem kopff oder stosß
ym in die brust

Another technique, called Over Running: when he binds against you at the staff, then fall over his right shoulder onto his neck with your point. If he means to set off the point with the other point of the staff, then strike quickly with your other point to his head, or jab to his chest.

59r

Aber ein stuck das geist das uber lauffen
won er dir angebunden hat an die stangen so
fall ym oder uber sin rechte achsel an den hals
mit dem ort wil er dan den ort ab setzen mit
dem andern ort der stangen so schlach schnel mit
dinem andern ort ym zu dem kopff oder stoß
ym in die brust

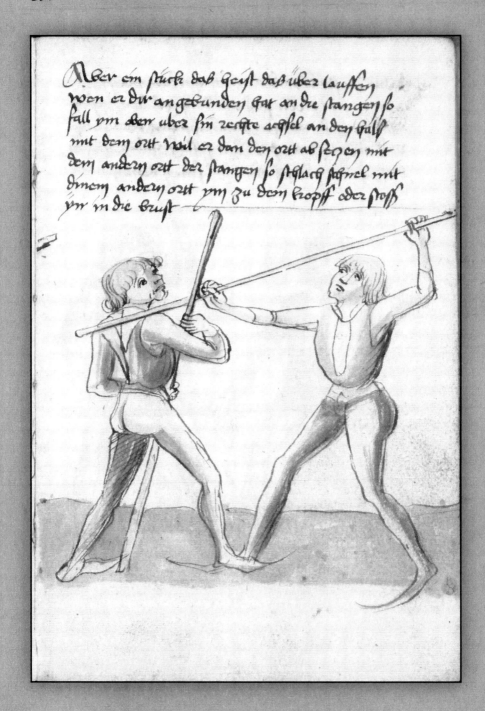

Aber ein stürtz yn der wyt von dem man furt
er einen schlag oder stoß uff dich zu dem gesicht
oder brust so ver satz vm den schlag oder stich
vnd nym einen stoß oder schlag wider gegen
yn zu dem koph oder zu° sinen benen

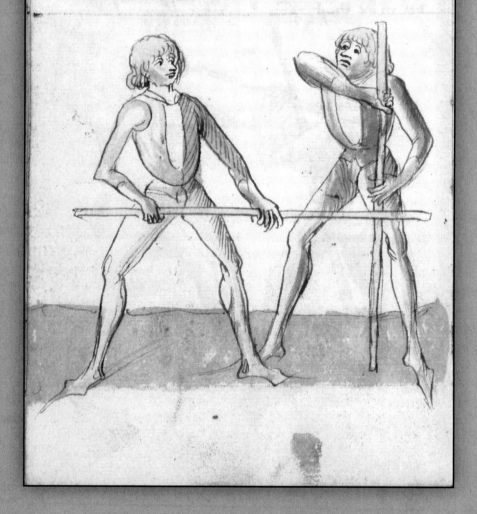

59v

Aber ein stück yn der wytt von dem man furt
er einem schlag oder stoß uff dich zů dem gesicht
oder brust so ver setz ym den schlag oder stich
und nym einen stoß oder schlag wider gegen
ym zu dem koph oder zů sinen benen

Another technique, at long distance from the opponent: if he delivers a blow or jab to your face or chest, then parry his blow or thrust, and execute a jab or blow in return to his head or legs.

Merck aber ein stück wen er dir schnel anbyndt
und du ym wider von oben so vasß sin stangen
zu der dinen und druck ym die finger so müß
er die stangen lassen faren daß heisset der
kloben

Note, another technique: when he binds you quickly, and you him in return from above, then pin his staff to yours and press his fingers so that he must let go of the staff. This is called the Clamp.

60r

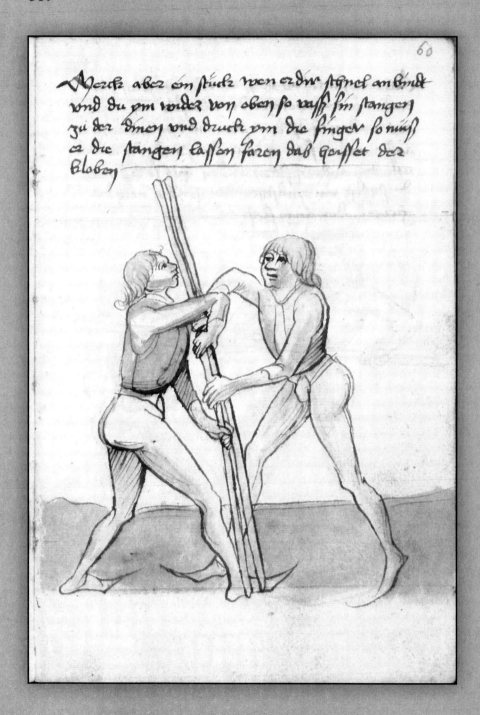

Aber ein stück das heist die uber winden mit
beiden örten welcher dir uberselt mit einem
ort an den halß dem soltu mit dem andern ort
auß winden selt er mit dem andern wider
uff die andern sitten an den halß so laß nitt
du stossest ym zwisschen den henden nach der
gurgel oder angesicht

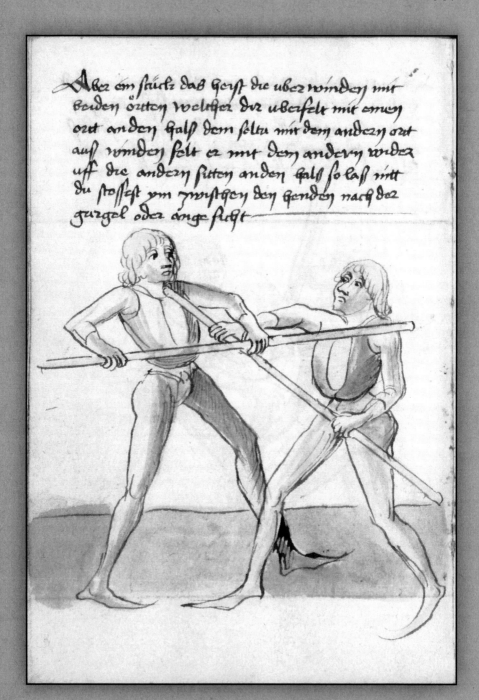

60v

Aber ein stück daß heist die uber winden mit
beiden ortten welcher dir uberfelt mit einen
ortt an den halß dem soltu mit dem andern ortt
auß winden felt er mit dem andern wider
uff die andern sitten an den halß so laß nitt
du stoffest ym zwischen den henden nach der
gurgel oder angesicht

Another technique, called Winding Over with both points: when someone falls over you with one point onto your neck, you should wind him out with the other point. If he falls with the other point on the other side onto your neck, then don't hesitate until you jab between his hands to the throat or face.

61r

Merck daß is ein besunder gut stück in der
stangen und heist daß under lauffen wen du
ein stangen hast und er ein schlecht er dir dan
nach den schenkeln oder lyb so lauff mit
dinem hindern ort dyner rechten sytten von
unden uff nach dem schlag und fall ym hoch uber
syn brust mit dem lincken arm und mit den
lincken fuß hinder die synen so wurffstu yn
nider

Note, this is a particularly good technique with the staff and is called
Under Running: when you have a staff and he has one, and he strikes
to your thigh or body, then run with your rear point on your right side
up from below after the blow and fall high over his breast with your left
arm, and with your left foot behind his, thus throwing him down.

61r

Merck das ist ein besunder gut stuck inder
stangen vnd heist das vnder lauffen wen du
ein stangen hast vnd er ein schlecht oder dar
nach den schenckeln oder lyb so lauff mit
dinem hindern ort dyner rechten seyten von
vnden uff nach dem schlag vnd fall ym hoch uber
sein brust mit dem lincken arm vnd mit dem
lincken fuss hinder die synen so wurffstu yn
inder

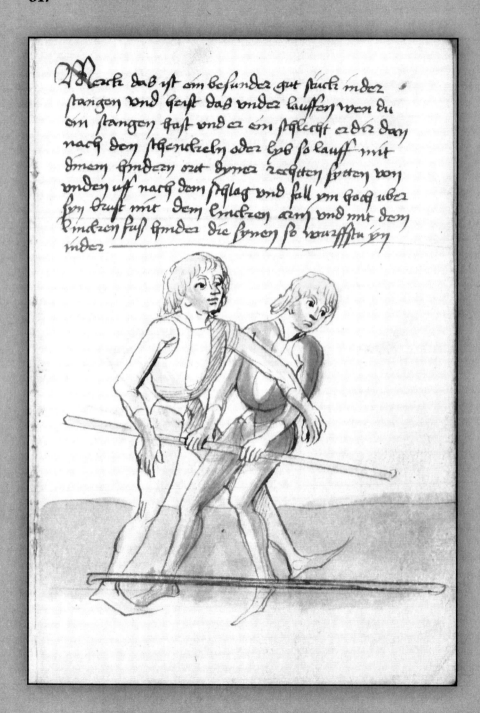

61v

Blank

62r • Poleaxe (ff. 62r–65r)

Merck daß ist auch ein leer wie du mit kemph //
licher wer solt wartten mordt agst und helle //
bartten daß ist auch zu dem kampff gericht
schleg stöß ringen macht zů nicht ~
Daß ist auch der text

Note this is also a lesson of how you should, with dueling weapons, act with the murder axe and the halberd, which is also for the judicial duel; striking, thrusting and wrestling counter-techniques.

This now is the text.

62r

Merck das ist auch ein leer wie du mit kempf
licher wer solt warten mordt agst vnd helle
barten das ist auch zu dem kampff gericht
schleg stöß ringen macht zu° mest

¶ Das ist auch der text

62v

Merck hastu ein mordtagst oder hellenbarten
in der hand und er auch ein so halt In vor dir
zwergß uff dinen beinen daß der linck fuß
vor stee und der spitz yn das gesicht schlecht er den uff
dich von oben oder furt ein stich so
var mit diner versatzüng und arbeit
auch als du wol weist mit dem
hudß end

Note, if you have a murder axe or halberd in the hand and he has one also, then hold it before you across your legs so that the left foot stands forward and the point is to his face. If he strikes to you from above or drives a thrust, then move with your parry and work as you also well know how to do with the butt[35] end.

---

[35] I cannot determine exactly what the word *hudß* means, but in context this must imply the tail of the axe.

Aber ein stuck schlect er dir hoch zů dem koph
so far hoch uff gewapnet und versetz ym dem schlag
wil er amsich ryssen dem schlag oder spytz solt
ym in daß gesicht wyssen mag dir daß nit gelingen
so under lauff yn recht mit ringen

Another technique: if he strikes high to you to the head, then drive high with the "armed hand" and parry his stroke. If he wants to pull towards him you shall turn the blow or the point into his face. If you cannot succeed with this, then run under it truly with wrestling.

63r

Aber ein sturtz schlecht er dir hoch zu dem kopff
so far hoch uff gewapnet vnd versetz ym dem schlag
vnd er amsich ryssen den schlag oder spytz solt
ym in das gesicht wyssen mag dir das mit gelingen
so vnder lauff ym recht mit zugen

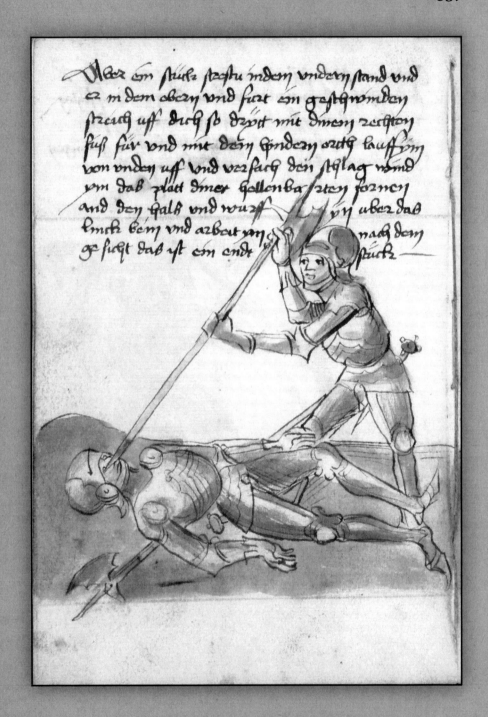

63v

Aber ein stuck steestu in dem undern stand und
er in dem obern und furt ein geschwinden
streich uff dich so drytt mit dinem rechten
fuß fur und mit dein hindern ortth lauff ym
von unden und verfach den schlag wind
ym daß platt diner hellenbarten fornen
und den halß und wurff yn uber daß
linck bein und arbeit ym nach dem
gesicht das ist ein endt stuck

Another technique: If you stand in the lower stance and he is in the upper [stance] and he drives with a fast strike to you, then step with your right foot forward and with the rear point run under it and catch the stroke. Wind the blade of your halberd forward and under the neck and throw him over the left leg and work to his face. This is a finishing technique.

Merck das stuck ist schlecht und gericht hastu
ein hellenbarten und er einen und stet gegen
dir mit gezogner wer und wil uff dich schlagen
so ste geschmügt mit diner hellenbarten an dein
lyb er schlach oben oder under so versetz ym den
schalg und uber wurff ym In hellenbarten
hinweg mit der din oder stich ym nach dem
gesicht daß ist güt

Note, this technique is simple and effective: If you have a halberd and
he has one and stands against you with the weapon drawn and wants
to strike to you, then stand with your halberd pressed at your body. If
he strikes above or below, then parry his stroke and throw his halberd
away with yours or thrust to his face, which is good.

64r

Aber ein stuck wil er dich werffen uber den
lincken fuß vnd hät dir die schist agst ander
halb gelert so far ym vnder sin elebogen
mit diner hellenbarten das das vnder end
uber sich kum vnd stoss ym oben von dir so
werstu ym den wurff

64v

Aber ein stück wil er dich werffen uber den
lincken füß und hat dir die strytt agst unden
halß gelert so far ym hinder sin ellebogen
mit diner hellenbarten daß daß under end
uber sich küm und stoß ym oben von dir so
werstu ym den wurff

Another technique: If he wants to throw you over the left foot and has placed the battle axe to your neck, then drive behind his elbow with your halberd so that the lower end comes upward, and push him above from you so that you defend the throw.

Merck das ist des besten stück eins sunder mit den
hellenbarten wen ir beid gogen einander stond
und keiner wil vor schlagen so fach an mit
ein grossen streich geet er dan uf mit der
vorsatzung so verzugk dne streich und stoß
ym zů dem lyb oder gesicht daß kan er nit
wol brechen und ist güt

Note that this is one of the very best techniques for the halberd: when you both stand against each other and no one wants to strike first, then prepare a great stroke. If he goes to parry it, then pull the stroke and thrust to his body or face. This he cannot counter well and that is good.

65r

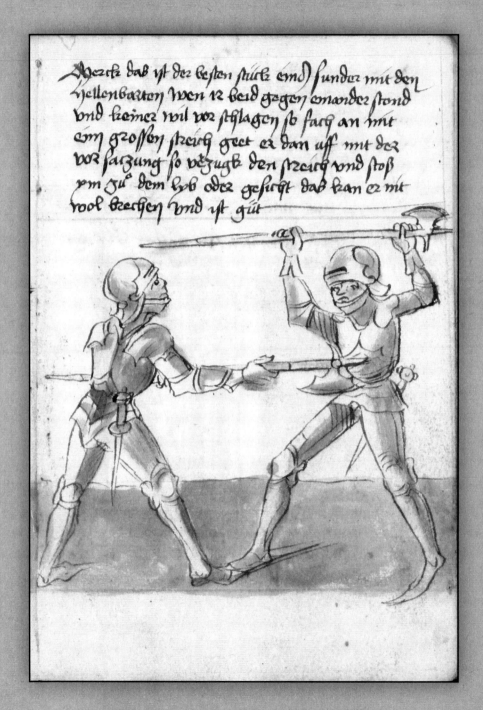

Merck das ist der besten stück eins sunder mit den
hellenbarten wen ir beid gegen einander stond
vnd keiner wil vor schlagen so fach an mit
ein grossen streich geet er dan uff mit der
vor satzung so verzugk den streich vnd stoß
ym zü dem lyb oder gesicht das kan er mit
wol brechen vnd ist güt

Merck das ist der frewleykh krampf wol
bewegt schilt kolben vnd tegen macht zu°
mecht Das ist der text
Hastu einen schilt vnd kolben vnd er auch
also vnd solten zamen dretten so halt den
schilt strackß wz dir ver wurfft er dan smen
kolben so trist nahen zu° im vnd schlag

im nach si men hen den ab er von
dem schilt mercht frommen das wer gut

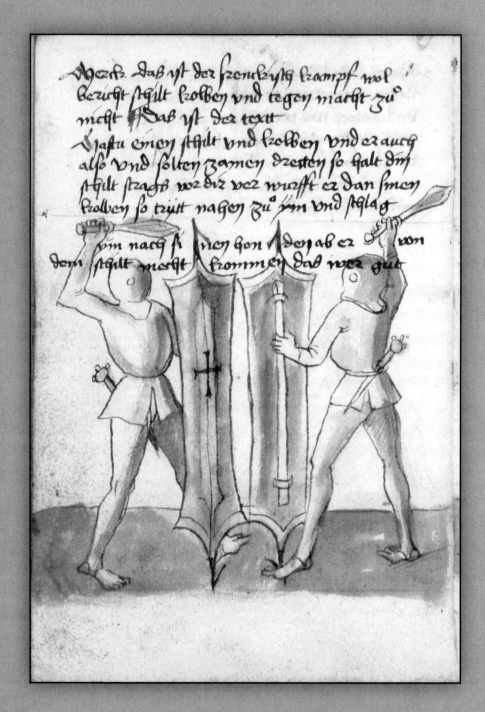

65v • *Franconian Rite Shield and Club Duel* (ff. 65v–67r)

Merck daß ist der frenckisch kampf wol
bericht schilt kolben und tegen macht zů
nicht Das is der text

Hastu einen schilt und kolben und er auch
also und solten zamen dretten so halt din
schilt stragß vor dir ver wurfft er dan sinen
kolben so trytt nahen zů ym und schlag
ym nach sinen henden ab er von
dem schilt mecht kommen daß wer güt

Note, this is an accurate report of the Franconian duel with shield, club and dagger counter-techniques. This is the text.

If you have a shield and club and he does as well, and should you both advance together, then hold your shield out in front of you. If he casts his club, then step near him and strike at his hands so that his shield comes away from him. This is good.

Aber ein stück mit dem langen schilt und
kolben haut er sin kolben fer schlagen oder
für worffen so ver wurff den din auch bald
und folg dem wurff nach und stoß ym
mit dein einem ortt zwischen sinem schilt
und lincken armß zů dem lyb oder
bring yn von dem schilt

Another technique with the long shield and club. If he strikes his club to hit or cast, then cast yours also quickly and follow after the throw and thrust with one of your points between his shield and left arm to the body or bring him from the shield.

66r

Aber ein stück mit dem langen schilt vnd
halben hatt es sin hochen fer schlagen oder
für werffen so ver wurff den dm auch bald
vnd folg dem wurff nach vnd stoß ym
mit dem einen ort zwischen sinem schilt
vnd lincken arm zu dem lyb oder
dring yn von dem schilt

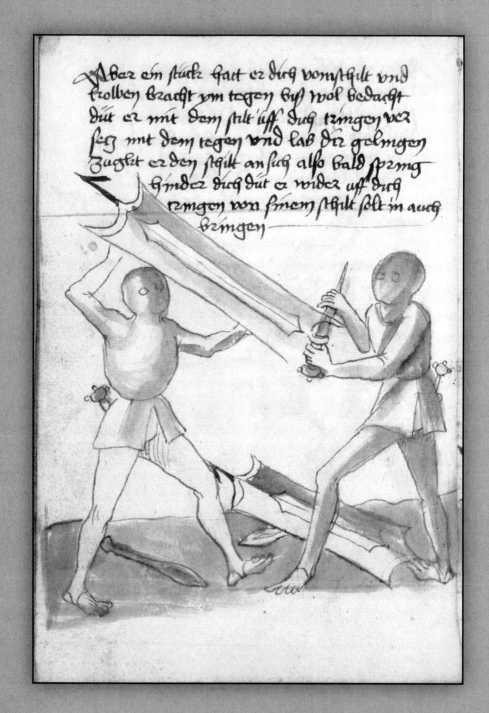

Aber ein stuck hait er dich von schilt vnd
kolben bracht ym tegen biß wol bedacht
düt er mit dem stilt uff dich ringen ver
setz mit dem tegen vnd laß dir gelingen
zuckt er den stilt an sich also bald spring
hinder dich düt er wider uff dich
ringen von sinem schilt solt in auch
bringen

66v

Aber ain stück hatt er dich vom schilt und
kolben bracht ym tegen biß wol bedacht
düt er mit dem scilt uff dich tringen ver
setz mit dem tegen und laß dir gelingen
zugkt er den schilt an sich also bald spring
hinder dich düt er wider uff dich
tringen von sinen schilt solt in also
bringen

Another technique. If he has brought you from the shield and club be well advised with the dagger. If he intends to press you with the shield then parry with the dagger and make sure you succeed. If he pulls the shield back to himself, then spring backward quickly. If he intends to again press you, you shall also bring him off of his shield.

67r

Wiltu geben end und haptt beid tegen in der
hend so soltu uff ym ein stich ver bringen
frölich laß dir gelingen ver setzt er den stich
und nympt dy dem ellebogen daß ge wicht
wider nym mach zů nicht also du wol weist

If you want to finish and you both have daggers in your hands, then you should bring forth a thrust freely to him and let yourself succeed. If he then parries the thrust and takes your balance by the elbow you take his in return. This counters, as you know well.

67r

Wiltu geben end vnd haptt beid tegen in der
herd so soltu uff yn em stich ver bzingen
frolich laß dir gelingen ver sezt er den stich
vnd nÿmpt by den elleboge das gerust
wider nÿm mach zu micht alß du wol weyst

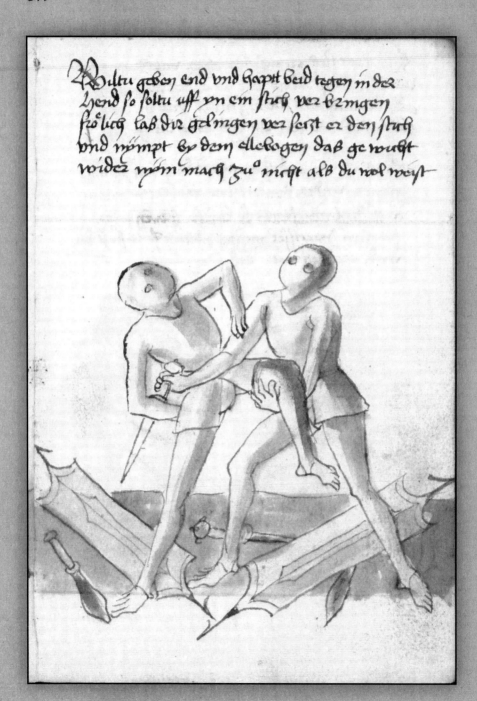

Hie hept sich an meyster peter valckmarß
kunst zů roß   Das erst mit der glenen
Darnach mit dem swert vnd in vngen
Das ist der text ein gemeine ler zu roß

Das ist die erst hut schutz dich mit diner
glenen vnder den rechten arm rent eran
auff dich mit sener so laß sy faxen in da
smitten wechßel vnder durch so ruffest du
vnd er dich mit   zů

67v • Roßfechten (ff. 67v–72v)

Hie hept sich an meister peter valcknerß
kunst zů roß Daß erst mit der glenen
Darnach mit dem swert und in ringen
Daß ist der text ein gemeine ler zu roß

Daß ist die erst hutt schick dich mit Diner
glenen under den rechten arm Rent er dan
auff dich mit sener so laß sy fornen nider
sincken wechsel unden Durch so triffest du
und er dich nit &c

Here begins Master Peter Falkner's art on horseback, first with the lance, thereafter with the sword and with wrestling. This is the text of a general lesson on horseback.

This is the first guard. Do this with your lance under the right arm. If he runs to you then with his, then let yours sink down before you and change through under so that you hit and his does not, etc.

Daß ist die ander hutt wen du zů ym ryrest
und er auff dich mit dem langen spyß so
leg din auff den lincken arm daß daß ysen
hindersich hangauff der lincken sytten
und strich schlecht auff an den synen und
da mit in daß gerist far auff yn So triffst
du und er nit Daß ist mit dem kurzen
spyß wider dem langen

This is the second guard. When you move to him and he does to you with the long spear, then place yours to the left arm so that the iron [spear tip] hangs backward on your left side and strike powerfully onto his and thus drive it up into the [lance] rest, so that yours hits and his does not. This is with the shortened spear against the long.

68r

Das ist die ander hutt wen du zů ym zij rest
vnd er auff dich mit dem langen spüs so
leg dm auff den lincken arm das das yſen
hindersich gang auff der lincken ſyten
vnd ſtuch ſchlecht auff an den hynen vnd
da mit in das gerist for auff yn So rufst
du vnd er mit Das ist mit dem kurtzen
ſpyß wider den langen

Die Trüt Hut renet er aber uff dich mit
dem langen spyß ſo ren auch gegen ym wider
alſo vnd wen du gerau zů ym kumſt ſo
laß dim ſpyß auß dem geryſt vallen mit dem
ſchafft in die erden vnd halt ym das yſen
an ſin ſpyß vnd ſetz ym da mit ab ſo rüſſt
du vnd er mit zc̃

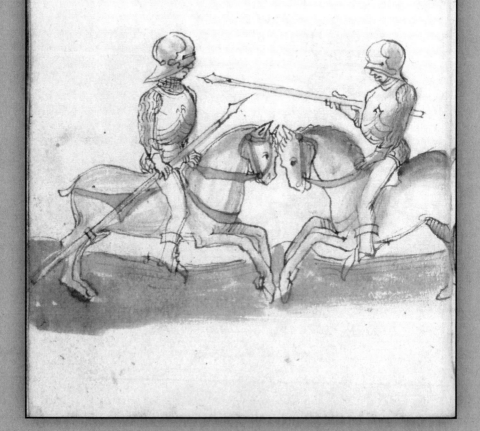

68v

Die Tritt hutt Rentt er aber uff dich mit
dem langen spyß so ren auch gegen ym wider
also und wen du genau zů ym kumst so
laß din spyß auß dem gerist vallen mit dem
schafft in die erden und halt ym daß ysen
an sin spyß und setz ym da mit ab so triffst
du und er nit &c

The third guard. If he runs again to you with the long spear then run also toward him and thus against and when you come close to him then let you spear fall from the [lance] rest with the shaft to the earth and hold the iron [spear tip] onto his spear and thereby set upon him so that you hit and he does not, etc.

Die vierd hutt bistu von dem spys komen
und hast din swert zogen renet er dan uff
dich mit dem langen spyß so leg din swert
dem pfert vornen uff den halß und setz
ym da mit ab und halt yn den ort in daß
gesicht daß ist gutt &c

The fourth guard. If you have come from the spear and have your sword drawn and he runs to you with the long spear, then place your sword in front on the horse's neck and with this set aside and hold the point to his face. This is good, etc.

69r

Die vierd hutt bistu von dem pferd komen
vnd hast din swert zogen rennet er dan vff
dich mit dem langen spiß so leg din swert
dem pfeart vornen vff den halß vnd setz
jm da mit ab vnd halt jm den ort in das
gesicht das ist gut ꝛc

Merck das ist ein besunder stuck mit dem
langen spys ist in der flucht es sy geteilt
oder flist so leg den spys uf die lincke
achsel und fluch für dich hinweg rent
er dir den nach und wil dir an setzen
in den rück so wend dich auf die lincke
siten gegen im und ritt mit im zü

69v

Merck daß ist ein besunder stuck mit dem
langen spyß bistu inder flucht eß sy gehiltz
oder sust so leg den spyß auff die lincke
achsel und fluch fur dich hinweg rent
er dir den nach und wil dir an setzen
in dem rück so wend dich auff dilinck
seiten gegen ym und triff mit ym &c

Note this is a particular technique for the long spear. If you are in flight, then place your spear on your left shoulder, either with the grip or otherwise, and flee forward and away. If he runs after you and wants to set upon you at the back then turn yourself to your left side against him and hit him [simultaneously] etc.

Hie hept sich an die kunst mit dem swert
zů roß Wiltu da mit meisterlich fechten
so soltu vor allen sachen wissen trei hutt

Die erst hut da leg din swert uff den lincke
arm haut er dan ein ober haw uff dich zů dem
koph so far hoch auff und ver setz ym den
streich sticht er aber dir zů dem gesicht so
ver setz ym ab mit der langen schnid vo~ diner
lincken syten an syn swert

Here begins the art of the sword on horseback. If you want to fight masterfully with it then you should know before all things the three guards.

The first guard. Place you sword on your left arm. If he strikes a stroke from above to your head, then drive up high and parry his strike. If he however thrusts to your face, then parry it away with the long edge from your left side onto his sword.

70r

Die ander hut halet din swert neben diner
rechten syten haut er den uff durch oder sticht
so stich von unden uff wider gegen ym zů dem
gesicht und vall ym mit dem gehiltz hoch uber
syn hand wind mit dem swert durch
und far sicz so nymstu ym das swert uß

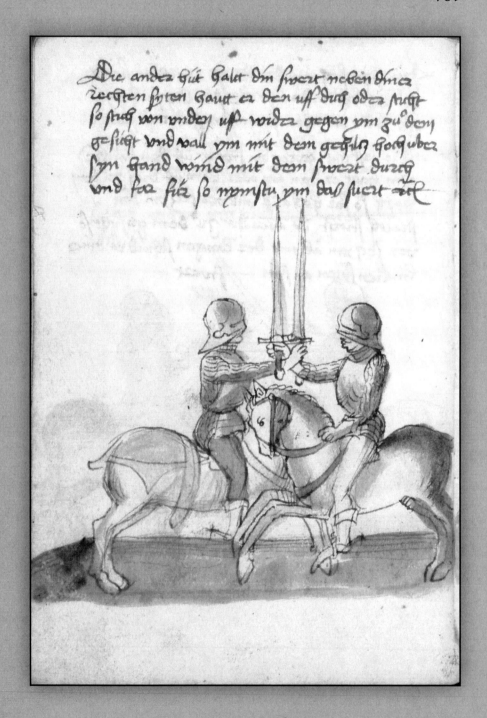

70v

Die ander hül haltt din swert neben diner
rechten sytten hautt er den auff dich oder sticht
so stich von under uff wider gegen ym zů dem
gesicht und vall ym mit dem gehiltz hoch uber
syn hand wind mit dem swert durch
und far für so nymstu ym daß swert &c

The second guard. Hold your sword next to your right side. If he strikes then to you or thrusts, then thrust from below up against him to the face and fall upon him with the hilt high over his hand, winding through with the sword and ride forward so that you take the sword etc.

Die drytt hütt stich er dir zů dem gesicht
so stich ym wider zů dem gesicht und fall y
m hoch mit dem knoph und hand uber syn
hand wind ym daß swert umb den
halß far für so wurffest yn herab daß ist
gut &c

The third guard. If he thrusts to your face, then thrust to his face too and fall upon him high with the pommel and hand over his hand and wind the sword around the neck, riding forward so that you throw him off. This is good, etc.

71r

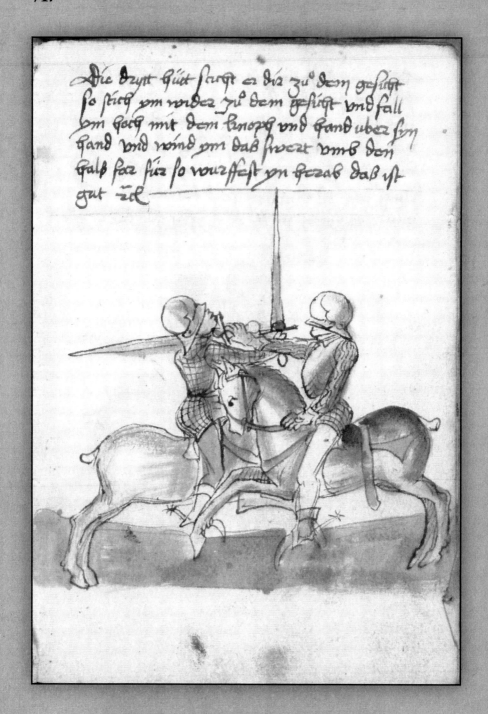

Merck das ist ein gut zingen vnd haist das
schloß zingen oder sunnen zaigen kumpt er
mit siner rechten syten an din lincken vnd
velt dir vnd den hals so slag von ynwen-
dig uber sinen arm od von uß wendig doch
kum mit de lincken hend der rechten zu
hilff oder nüm yn by dem ysin hut das ist gut

71v

Merck daß is ein gůt ringen und heisl daß
schloß ringen oder sunnen zeigen kumpt er
mit syner rechten sytten an din lincken und
velt dir umb den halß so slag von ynwen //
dig uber synen arm od von ußwendig doch
kum mit de~ lincken hend der rechten zů
hilff oder nym yn by dem ysen hüt da daß ist gůt

Note, this is a good wrestling technique and is called "lock wrestling" or the "sun pointer." If he comes with his right side to your left and falls around your neck, then strike from inside over his arm or from outside. Support your right hand with the left, or take him by the helmet. That is good.

Merck daß ist ein besunder gut stuck rytt er
dich under augen an und wil mit dir arbeiten
und felt dir umb den halß so begreiff syn
rechte hand mit dyner lincken und far mit
dinen rechten arm über syn und begryff
den sattelbogen daß heisset der schaff griff
oder gryff in mit diner rechten hand zwischen
sainen henden in den zaüm und ruck ubersich
so vellet er mit pfferd und mit dall

Note, this is a particularly good technique. If he rides to you, under
the eyes, and wants to work against you by falling around your neck,
then grab his right hand with your left and drive your right arm over
his and grab the saddle bow. This is called the Sheep Grip. Or, grab in
with your right hand between his hands to the bridle and jerk upward
so that he falls with the horse and with fury.

72r

Ist er ab getrungen oder geffallen so fall auch
ab von dem pfert vnd arbeit snell in
dem zingen als du wol waist felt er uff
den rucke so besteig süß in mit einem bein
mit dem ander in uff einen arm vnd
arbeit mit dem suert oder degen so er
ergot er sich

72v

Ist er ab getrungen oder gefallen so fall aüch
ab von dem pfertt und arbeit schnel in
dem ringen als du wol weist felt er uff
den rück so beschlüß in mit einen bein
mit dem andern uff einen arm und
arbeit mit de~ swert oder degen so er
gypt er sich

If he has been forced off or fallen, then dismount also from your horse and work quickly with the wrestling as you well know. If he falls to his back then contain him with a leg with the other on his arm and work with the sword or dagger so that he gives up.

73r

Blank

73r

Blank

Inside back cover

Blank

GLOSSARY

Pronunciation Key

[a:]	f*a*ther		[y]	pronounced like [i], but with the lips rounded
[ai]	w*i*fe, h*i*gh			
[e:]	s*ay*		[y:]	r*u*se
[ɛ]	b*e*t		[j]	*y*ear
[ə]	*a*bout, comm*o*n		[ç]	lo*ch*, but pronounced in the front of the mouth
[i:]	m*ee*t			
[u:]	b*oo*t		[x]	lo*ch*, but pronounced in the throat
[ö]	l*o*ng		[ŋ]	si*ng*
[o:]	h*o*le		[ʃ]	*sh*e

Abnehmen [ˈapne:mən] – (Taking off) A sudden departure from a bind whereby one's sword is freed to strike to the other side. Similar in meaning to *Zucken*.

Abschneiden [ˈapʃnaidən] – (Cutting off) Slicing cuts, delivered from above or below. One of the *Drei Wunder* (Three Wounders).

Absetzen [ˈapzetsən] – (Setting aside) To deflect a thrust or stroke at the same time as thrusting. The word can also denote a type of parry wherein the opponent's blade slides off of one's own.

Alber [ˈalbər] – (The Fool) One of the four primary guards in Liechtenauer's longsword fighting system. In it the sword is held with the hilt low and the blade angled 45 degrees with the point to the ground. It is a guard that invites an opponent's attack.

After – see *Nach*.

Am Schwert [am ˈʃve:rt] – (At the Sword) Techniques performed while remaining in a bind with an opponent's sword.

Ansetzen [ˈanzetsən] – (Setting Upon) To attack with the point.

Ausser Abnehmen [ˈausər ˈapne:mən] – (Outer taking) A type of *Nachreisen* (Traveling After) that is done by keeping your blade on the outside of the opponent's blade.

Aventail – A drape of mail armour attached to the bottom of a helmet, providing protection for the neck, throat and collar.

Bascinet – The most common knightly helmet of the 14th century.

Before – see *Vor.*

Besagew – Disc-shaped plate protecting an armoured man's armpit.

Bevor – A piece of plate armour defending the chin and neck.

Binden ['bindən] – (Binding) The act of making contact between two swords or other weapons.

Blosse ['bloːs] – an opening or target area. In unarmoured combat (*Blossfechten*), there are four openings: two (left and right) above the belt, and two below it.

Bloßfechten ['bloːsfɛçtən] – (Exposed Fighting) unarmoured combat.

Bruch ['brux] – (Break) A counter-technique, something that breaks an attack.

Buckler – A small shield, usually round, used for foot combat.

Buffalo – see *Buffel.*

Buffel ['byfəl] – (Buffalo) Period slang term for a cloddish fighter who relies only on strength.

Couter – Plate armour for the elbow.

Crown – see *Kron.*

Cuirass – Plate armour for the torso, comprising a breastplate and backplate en suite.

Cuisse – A piece of plate armour defending the thigh.

Displacement – see *Versetzen.*

Donnerschlag ['dönərʃlaːk] – (Thunder Stroke) See *Schlachenden Ort.*

Drei Ringen ['drai 'riŋən] – (Three Wrestlings) Three basic throwing or takedown techniques found in the Ringeck Fechtbuch.

Drei Wunder ['drai 'vundər] – (Three Wounders) The three ways of injuring an opponent with a longsword: thrusting, slicing, or striking. All three may be performed from each of the eight windings (*Acht Winden*).

Duplieren [du'pliːrən] – (Doubling) An attack made from a bind wherein one winds the sword behind the opponent's blade to strike or slice him in the face.

Durchlaufen [durçlaufən] – (Running through) Wrestling technique performed in longsword fighting in which one "runs through" the enemy's attack to grapple with him.

Durchstechen [durçʃtɛçən] – (Thrusting through) Technique performed in half-sword fighting where one thrusts down between the opponent's sword and his body.

Durchwechseln [durçʃvɛksəl] – (Changing through) Techniques for escaping from a bind by sliding one's point out from under an opponent's blade to thrust to another opening.

Fehler ['fe:lər] – (Feint) A deception with the sword that causes an opponent to commit to the defense of one opening while one's intent is to actually attack another opening.

Fühlen ['fy:lən] – (Feeling) The skill of sensing the degree of pressure exerted by one's opponent in a bind. One should determine how to react to an opponent by sensing whether he is "hard" or "soft" at the sword.

Gambeson – A thickly padded coat that sometimes served as a foundation for other armour components, sometimes covered elements of armour and at other times was used as a defense on its own.

Gauntlets – Plate armour defenses for the hands.

Glossa – Commentaries or gloss made by Sigmund Ringeck, Peter von Danzig, Jud Lew and Hans Speyer (and other masters, in various fechtbücher) that explain the meaning of Johannes Liechtenauer's cryptic verses (*Merkeverse*).

Greave – Plate armour piece for the lower leg.

Halbschwert [halpʃve:rt] – (Half-Sword) Method of wielding a longsword where the right hand holds the grip of the sword while the left grasps the mid-point of the blade. In this method, the sword can be wielded as a short thrusting spear or, with the pommel forward, as an implement with which to hook your opponent and throw him down. Also appears in Ringeck's manuscript as Kurzen Schwert, or "shortened sword."

Half-Sword – see *Halb Schwert*.

Hard – see *Hart*.

Harnischfechten ['harniʃfɛçtən] – (Harness fighting) Armoured combat, usually implying foot combat in harness.

Hart [hart] – (Hard) Condition in a bind where one is pressing strongly against an opponent's blade.

Hau [hau] – (Hew or Stroke) A stroke or hewing blow with a sword.

Haubergeon – A shorter version of the earlier *hauberk*, or tunic of mail. Haubergeons usually came down to the middle of the thigh and could have long or short sleeves.

Hende Drucken [hant drukən] – (Pressing of the Hands) Slicing technique where one slices under an opponent's hands as he attacks from above, then winds the sword's edge so as to slice down onto his hands, thereby pushing the opponent aside.

Hengen – see *Zwei Hengen.*

Hut [huːt] – see *Leger.*

Indes [inˈdɛs] – (Instantly, During, or Meanwhile) Term describing the act of responding almost simultaneously to an opponent's actions, whether using one of the "Five Strokes" to counter a stroke or reacting in a bind based on the degree of blade pressure being exerted by the opponent. This quick reaction, performed during an opponent's action, facilitates one's transition from a defensive mode (*Nach*) to an offensive one (*Vor*).

Krieg [kriːk] – (War) The second phase of a fighting encounter, when the combatants have moved to close combat range. The techniques used in this close combat are limited to those associated with winding (*Winden*) and wrestling at the sword (*Ringen am Schwert*).

Kron [ˈkroːn] – (the Crown) A defensive position wherein one raises the longsword, point upward, to intercept a downward blow on the hilt. Once the attack has been caught, one can rush in to grapple with the opponent.

Krumphau [ˈkrumphau] – One of Liechtenauer's five strokes, directed diagonally downward from one's right side to the opponent's right side, such that the hands are crossed, or from the left side with the hands uncrossing as the stroke is executed. It is usually directed against an opponent's hands or the flat of his sword. The name derives from the crooked trajectory of the blow—*krump* means twisted—as the sword travels across one's person. The Krumphau counters the guard *Ochs*, as it closes off that guard's line of attack.

Kurzen Schneide [ˈkyrtsən ˈʃnaidə] – (Short Edge) The back edge of a longsword. When a sword is held out with the point facing an opponent, this edge is the one that is facing up.

Langenort [ˈlaŋənort] – (the Long Point) A secondary guard described by Ringeck. It is much like the guard Pflug (the Plow) except that the hands are extended forward so as to menace an opponent's face at longer range.

Langen Schneide [ˈlaŋən ˈʃnaidə] – (Long Edge) The true edge of a longsword. When a sword is held out with the point facing an opponent, this edge is the one that is facing down.

Langen Schwert [ˈlaŋən ˈʃveːrt] – (Longsword) A late medieval hand-and-a-half sword, usually with a sharply tapering point that is suited to thrusting attacks. The longsword is the weapon that Liechtenauer's teachings focus most on.

Long Edge – see *Langen Schneide.*

Longsword – see *Langen Schwert.*

Leger ['le:gər] – A guard or fighting stance. Liechtenauer's system specifies the use of four guards (see also *Vier Leger*), but other masters, later added other positions to the system.

Liechtenauer, Johannes ['li:çtənauər, jo'hanəs] – German fight master who flourished in the 14th century. After studying with other masters throughout Europe, Liechtenauer synthesized his own system of fighting which he ensconced in cryptic verse (*Merkverse*). These teachings were included in the works of many subsequent masters and informed German swordsmanship for over 200 years.

Mail – Armour composed of interwoven rings of iron or steel, forming a flexible defense nearly impervious to cuts.

Meisterhaue ['maistərhau] – (Master Strokes) Name for the five secret strokes of Johannes Liechtenauer's system of longsword fighting. These sword strokes are designed to defend against an opponent's attack while counterattacking him.

Merkeverse ['mɛrkfɛrs] – (Teaching Verse) The cryptic verses of Master Johannes Liechtenauer, which were written to obscure their meaning to the uninitiated and serve as a series of mnemonics to those schooled in his fighting system.

Messer ['mɛsər] – A short, falchion-like single-handed sword. The word, which means "knife," may also be another name for a dagger.

Mittelhau ['mitəlhau] – (Middle Stroke) Any horizontal blow, usually directed to an opponent's mid-section.

Mortschlag ['mortʃla:k] – (Murder Stroke) See *Schlachenden Ort.*

Mortstöße ['mortʃto:s] – (Murder Strikes) Blows with hand used to stun an opponent as a prelude to grappling with him.

Mutieren [mu'ti:rən] – (Transmuting) A longsword technique, employed from a bind, whereby one winds the sword so that one's point comes down on the opposite side on the opponent's blade to thrust to a lower opening.

Nach [na:x] – (After) The defensive principle in Liechtenauer's system. When one is forced to respond to an adversary's attack, one is fighting in the After. As it is imperative that one regain the initiative, one employs techniques from the After to get back to fighting in the Before—that is, on the offensive.

Nachreisen ['na:xraizən] – (Traveling After, Chasing, Following) Methods for out-timing your adversary's attack so that you can return to fighting offensively. One can strike right after a missed stroke by your opponent, or right before he strikes, for instance.

Nebenhut [ˈneːbən huːt] – (Near Guard) Secondary guard position where one holds the sword at either side of the body with the point trailing slightly backward. The name derives from the sword being near the leg.

Oberhau [ˈoːbərhau] – (Stroke from Above) A stroke directed downward from above, either diagonally or vertically.

Oberschnitt [ˈoːbərʃnit] – (Slice from Above) A slicing cut that pushes downward from the guard Pflug on either side.

Ochs [ŏks] – (the Ox) One of Liechtenauer's four primary guards. The sword is held with the hands crossed high at the right side of the head, with the point directed down towards the opponent's face and the left leg leading. There is also left side version of this guard where the sword is held with the hands uncrossed, with the right leg leading.

Pauldron – Piece of plate armour defending the shoulder.

Parry – see *Versetzen*.

Pfobenzagel [ˈpfobəntsaːgəl] – (the Peacock's Tail) A method similar to the Wheel (*Redel*, see below).

Pflug [ˈpfluːk] – (the Plow) One of Liechtenauer's four primary guards. The sword is held with the hands crossed at the right side, the hilt at the right hip, with the point directed up towards the opponent's face and the left leg leading. There is also left side version of this guard where the sword is held with the hands uncrossed, with the right leg leading.

Poleyn – Piece of armour defending the knee.

Redel [ˈreːdəl] – (Wheel) A technique where the point is rotated around the opponent's sword, like the motion of a wheel, until an opening to attack with the point if found.

Ringen am Schwert [ˈriŋən am ˈʃveːrt] – (Wrestling at the Sword) Techniques for grappling in a bind in longsword combat. These are grouped under *Durchlaufen*, one of Liechtenauer's primary techniques.

Roundel – 1) Disc-shaped parts forming the guard and pommel of a Roundel dagger. 2) Circular plate covering the armpit on a fully armoured man, also called a besagew.

Roßfechten [ˈrösfɛçtən] – (Horse Combat) Liechtenauer's mounted combat in armour.

Sabaton – Plate armour piece covering the foot.

Sallet – Helmet common throughout much of the 15th century.

Scheitelhau [ˈʃaitəlhau] – (Scalp or Parting Stroke) One of Liechtenauer's five strokes, a vertical stroke from above with the long edge aimed at the opponent's head or upper chest. It counters the guard *Alber* by means of superior range. The name derives from the primary target of this stroke, the scalp.

Schielhau [ˈʃiːlhau] – (Squinting Stroke) One of Liechtenauer's five strokes, a vertical stroke from above with the short edge aimed at the opponent's right shoulder. It counters the guard Pflug by closing of its line of attack. The name derives from the position of the person striking—one turns such that one is "squinting" at the opponent with only one eye.

Schlachenden Ort [ˈʃlaxəndən ˈȯrt] – (Battering Point) Strikes with the pommel, delivered against an armoured opponent with both hands on the blade. Also called *Mortschlag* and *Donnerschlag*.

Schnitt [ʃnit] – (Cut) Slicing cuts made with either edge of the longsword. One of the *Drei Wunder* (Three Wounders). There are four basic cuts: two directed from above, using a position corresponding to the guard Pflug, and two directed from below, from a position like the guard Ochs.

Schranckhut [ˈʃraŋhuːt]– (Barrier Guard) A secondary guard that figures in later master's commentaries but not in Liechtenauer's verse. To stand in the guard you either lead with your right leg with your sword hanging diagonally down almost to the ground on your left side, or lead with your left leg with your sword hanging diagonally down on your right side.

Schwech [ˈʃɛçv]– (Weak) The part of a longsword blade extending from the middle of the blade to the point. You can not bind strongly on this part of the sword.

Schwert Nehmen [ˈʃveːrt ˈneːmən] – (Sword Taking) Binding and grappling techniques designed to disarm the opponent swordsman.

Setting Aside – see *Absetzen*.

Short Edge – see *Kurzen Schneide*.

Sprechfenster [ˈʃprɛːçfɛnstər] – (Speaking Window) One of the techniques of *Zwei Hengen* (Two Hangers). After binding with an opponent's sword, you remain in the bind with your arms extended in the guard *Langenort*. From this position you wait and sense his actions through changes in blade pressure (*Fühlen*). Thus, your adversary's intent is "spoken" through the "window" created by the bind.

Starcke [ʃtark]– (Strong) The part of a longsword blade that extends from the crossguard to the middle of the blade. One can bind with strength on this part of the blade.

Strong – see *Starcke*.

Stück [ʃtyk] – (Piece) A technique or series of techniques strung together.

Twerhau (see, *Zwerchhau*)

Überlaufen ['y:bərlaufən] – (Overrunning) Techniques whereby one outreaches an opponent's low stroke or thrust with a high stroke or thrust. One of Liechtenauer's primary techniques, it also includes methods for reaching over and pulling down an opponent's blade as he attacks high.

Unterhalten ['untərhaltən] – (Holding Down) Wrestling techniques used for holding an opponent once he has been thrown to the ground.

Unterhau ['untərhau] – (Stroke from Below) A stroke directed upward from below, either diagonally or vertically.

Unterschnitt ['untərʃnit] – (Slice from Below) A slicing cut that pushes upward from the guard *Ochs* on either side.

Vambrace – A plate armour defense for the forearm. Sometimes this term refers to the entire arm defense.

Verkehrer [fɛr'ke:rər] – (Inverter) A technique performed while in a bind by inverting the position of the hilt so that the right thumb is situated beneath the sword. This brings the hilt high while the point menaces the opponent's face.

Versetzen ['fɛrzetsən] – (Parrying) To parry or block. Liechtenauer's teachings advise against using purely defensive displacements, as they allow one's opponent to maintain the initiative. A proper parry in Liechtenauer's system must contain an offensive component.

Vom Tag ['fŏm ta:k] – (From the Roof) One of Liechtenauer's four primary guards, designed primarily as starting position for strong strokes. One stands leading with the left leg, with the sword held at either the right shoulder or over the head. The guard can also be held at the left shoulder with the right leg leading.

Vom Schwert ['fŏm ʃve:rt] – (From the Sword) Term describing actions that involve removing one's sword from a bind.

Vor ['fo:r] – (Before) The offensive principle in Liechtenauer's system. As the control of initiative in the fight is all-important, one should seek to strike before an opponent does, so that the opponent is forced to remain on the defensive. Many of Liechtenauer's teachings describe methods for regaining the initiative if it has been lost momentarily.

Weak – see *Schwech*.

Weich [vaiç] – (Soft) Condition in a bind where one is exerting little pressure against an opponent's blade.

Winden ['vindən] – (Winding) A hallmark of Liechtenauer's fighting system, these are techniques where the sword or spear winds or turns about it long axis while binding an opponent's weapon. Winding is used to regain leverage in the bind and to seek out targets by changing the angle of attack without exposing a weakness in one's defense. There are eight basic windings, four performed while binding in the guard *Ochs* and four while binding in the guard *Pflug*. *Duplieren* and *Mutieren* are also types of winding.

Zornhau ['tsörnhau] – (Stroke of Wrath) One of Liechtenauer's five strokes, a diagonal stroke from above. It is so named because it is a powerful stroke that an enraged man would instinctively employ.

Zucken ['tsukən] – (Pulling or Withdrawing) The act of jerking one's weapon out of a bind to attack another opening.

Zufechten [tsu:'fɛçtən] – (the Approach) The first phase of combat, where one closes with the opponent.

Zůlauffend Ringen [tsu:'laufənd 'riŋən] – (Wrestling While Closing) Grappling techniques applied while approaching an opponent.

Zwerchhau ['tsvɛrçhau] – (Cross Stroke) One of Liechtenauer's five strokes, struck horizontally to the left side of the opponent's head using the short edge. If struck to an opponent's right side, the long edge is used. The Zwerchhau counters the guard *vom Tag*, as it closes off the line of attack of strokes from above.

Zwei Hengen [tsvai hɛŋən] – (Two Hangers) Positions in which the swords bind. One is where one's sword is held in the bind so that the pommel hangs down with the point menacing the opponent's face. This corresponds with the guard *Pflug*. The other is where the point hangs down from above to threaten the face, which corresponds with the guard *Ochs*.

BIBLIOGRAPHY

Primary Sources

Anonymous, *Hausbuch* (1389), Codex Hs. 3227a, German National Museum, Nuremburg.

Anonymous, *Fechtbuch* (ca. 1430), Ms. KK 5013, Kunsthistorisches Museum, Vienna, Austria.

Anonymous, *Fechtbuch* (15th c.), Cod. Guelf. 78.2 Aug. 20, Herzog August Bibliothek, Wolfenbüttel, Germany.

Anonymous, *Fechtbuch* (15th c.), Cod. Vindob. B 11093, Österreichische Nationalbibliothek, Vienna, Austria.

Anonymous, *Fechtbuch* (ca. 1500), Cod. 862, Fürstl. Fürstenbergische Hofbibliothek, Donaueschingen, Germany.

Anonymous, *Fechtbuch* (after 1500), Libr. Pict. A83, Staatsbibliothek Preußischer Kulturbesitz, Berlin, Germany.

Anonymous, *Gladiatoria* (1st half of 15th c.), MS. germ. quart. 16, Jagelonische Bibliothek, Krakau, Poland.

Anonymous, *Goliath* (1st quarter of 16th c.), MS. germ. quart. 2020, Jagelonische Bibliothek, Krakau, Poland.

Czynner, Hans, *Fechtbuch* (1538), Ms. 963, Universitätsbibliothek, Graz, Austria.

von Danzig, Peter, *Fechtbuch* (1452), Codex 44 A 8, Library of the National Academy, Rome, Italy.

von Eyb, Ludwig, *Kriegsbuch* (c. 1500), Ms. B 26, Universitätsbibliothek Erlangen, Germany.

Falkner, Peter, *Fechtbuch* (end of 15th c.), Ms. KK 5012, Kunsthistorisches Museum, Vienna, Austria.

Kal, Paulus, *Fechtbuch* (c. 1470), CGM 1507, Bayerische Staatsbibliothek, Munich, Germany.

Kal, Paulus, *Fechtbuch* (late 15th c. copy), Cod. S554, Zentralbibliothek, Solothurn, Switzerland.

Kal, Paulus, *Fechtbuch* (late 15th c. copy), Ms. KK 5126, Kunsthistorisches Museum, Vienna, Austria.

Lecküchner, Johannes (1478), *Fechtbuch*, Cod. Pal. Germ. 430, Universitätsbibliothek Heidelberg, Germany.

Lecküchner, Johannes (1482), *Fechtbuch*, Cgm. 582, Bayerische Staatsbibliothek, Munich, Germany.

(Jud) Lew, *Fechtbuch* (c. 1450), Cod.I.6.4°.3, Universitätsbibliothek Augsburg, Germany.

Liberi da Premariacco, Fiore dei, *Fior Battaglia* (1409), MS Ludwig XV.13, Getty Museum, Los Angeles, USA.

Mair, Paulus Hector, *Fechtbuch* (1542), Mscr. Dresd. C93 / 94, Sächsische Landesbibliothek, Dresden, Germany.

Mair, Paulus Hector, *Fechtbuch* (1542), Cod. Vindob. 10825 / 26, Österreichische Nationalbibliothek, Vienna, Austria.

Meyer, Joachim, *Grundtliche beschreibung der freyen ritterlichen und adelichen kunst des fechtens* (A Thorough Description of the Free, Knightly and Noble Art of Fencing). Strasbourg, 1570.

Ringeck, Sigmund, *Fechtbuch* (c.1440), Dresden, State Library of Saxony, Ms. Dresd. C 487.

von Speyer, Hans, *Fechtbuch* (1491), M I 29, Universitätsbibliothek Salzburg, Germany.

Sutor, Jakob, *New Künstliches Fechtbuch* (1612), Frankfurt am Main, Germany.

Talhoffer, Hans, *Fechtbuch*, (1443), Ms. Chart. A558, Forschungsbibliothek Gotha, Germany.

Talhoffer, Hans, *Fechtbuch*, (1450?), HS XIX, 17-3, Gräfl. Schloss Königseggwald, Germany.

Talhoffer, Hans, *Fechtbuch* (1459), Thott 290 2°, Königliche Bibliothek, Copenhagen, Denmark.

Talhoffer, Hans, *Fechtbuch* (1467), Cod. icon. 394a, Bayerische Staatsbibliothek, Munich, Germany.

Wilhalm, Jörg, *Fechtbuch* (1522/23), CGM 3711, Bayerische Staatsbibliothek, Munich, Germany.

Wilhalm, Jörg, *Fechtbuch* (1556), CGM 3712, Bayerische Staatsbibliothek, Munich, Germany.

Secondary Sources

Amberger, J. Christoph, *The Secret History of the Sword*. Baltimore, Maryland, Hammerterz Verlag, 1996.

Anglo, Sydney, *The Martial Arts of Renaissance Europe*. London and New Haven, Yale, 2000.

Arano, Luisa Cogliati, *The Medieval Health Handbook: Tacuinum Sanitatis*. New York, George Braziller, 1976.

Arnold, Benjamin, *German Knighthood 1050-1300*. Oxford University Press, 1985.

————, *Princes and Territories in Medieval Germany*, Cambridge University Press, 1991.

Blair, Claude, *European Armour*. London, B. T. Batsford Ltd., 1958.

Edge, David and John Miles Paddock, *Arms and Armour of the Medieval Knight*. New York, Crescent Books, 1988.

Forgeng, Jeffrey L., *The Medieval Art of Swordsmanship: A Facsimile & Translation of Europe's Oldest Personal Combat Treatise, Royal Armouries MS. I.33*. Union City, California and Leeds, UK, Chivalry Bookshelf/Royal Armouries, 2003.

Galas, S. Matthew, "Kindred spirits: The art of the sword in Germany and Japan," published in the *Journal of Asian Martial Arts*, VI (1997), pp. 20 - 46

Hils, Hans-Peter, *Master Johann Liechtenauer's kunst des langen schwerts*. Frankfurt am Main, 1985.

Liberi da Premariacco, Fiore dei, *Flos duellatorum in arnis, sine arnis, equester, pedester*, Francesco Novati, ed., Bergamo, 1902.

Lindholm, David, and Peter Svärd, *Sigmund Ringeck's Knightly Art of the Longsword*. Boulder, Colorado, Paladin Press, 2003.

Oakeshott, R. Ewart, *The Archeology of Weapons*. Woodbridge, UK, Boydell, 1960.

————, *The Sword in the Age of Chivalry*. London, UK, Arms & Armour Press, 1964.

————, *European Weapons and Armour*. N. Hollywood, California, Beinfeld Publishing, 1980.

Porzio, Luca and Gregory Mele, *Arte Gladiatoria Dimicandi: 15th Century Swordsmanship of Master Filippo Vadi*. Union City, California, Chivalry Bookshelf, 2002.

Talhoffer, Hans, *Medieval Combat: A Fifteenth-Century Illustrated Manual of Swordfighting and Close-Quarter Combat*. Edited Mark Rector, London, Greenhill Books, 2000.

Tobler, Christian Henry, *Fighting with the German Longsword*. Union City, California, Chivalry Bookshelf, 2004.

————, *In Saint George's Name*. Wheaton, Illinois, Freelance Academy Press, 2010.

————, *In Service of the Duke: The 15ᵗʰ Century Fighting Treatise of Paulus Kal*. Highland Village, Texas, Chivalry Bookshelf, 2006.

————, *Secrets of German Medieval Swordsmanship: Sigmund Ringeck's Commentaries on Johannes Liechtenauer's Verse*. Union City, California, Chivalry Bookshelf, 2001.

Wagner, Paul and Stephen Hand, *Medieval Sword and Shield: The Combat System of Royal Armouries MS I.33*. Union City, California, Chivalry Bookshelf, 2003.

Waldburg Wolfegg, Christoph Graf zu, *Venus and Mars: The World of the Medieval Housebook*. Munich and New York, Prestel, 1998.

Waldman, John, *Hafted Weapons in Medieval and Renaissance Europe*. Leiden, Netherlands and Boston, USA, Brill, 2005.

Welle, Rainer, *"...und wisse das alle hobischeit kompt von deme ringen": Der Ringkampf als adelige Kunst im 15. und 16. Jahrhundert Eine Sozialhistorische Und Bewegungsbiographische Interpretation Aufgrund Der Handschriftlichen Und Gedruckten Ringlehren Des Spatmittelalters*, 1993.

Wierschin, Martin, *Meister Johann Liechtenauers kunst des fechtens*. Munich, Muenchener Text und Untersuchungen zur deutschen Literatur des Mittelalters, 1965.

Zabinski, Grzegorz with Bartlomiej Walczak, *Codex Wallerstein: A Medieval Fighting Book on the Longsword, Falchion, Dagger, and Wrestling*. Boulder, Colorado, Paladin Press, 2002.

Ziegler, Vickie L., *Trial by Fire and Battle in Medieval German Literature*. Woodbridge, UK, Camden House, 2004.